WESTWARD THE WOMEN

BY

NANCY WILSON ROSS

AYER COMPANY PUBLISHERS, INC.
SALEM, NEW HAMPSHIRE 03079

Reprint Edition, 1987
AYER Company, Publishers, Inc.

Reprinted from a copy in
The Library, University of Illinois
at Urbana-Champaign

Manufactured in the United States of America

ISBN 0-8369-1846-0

WESTWARD THE WOMEN

WESTWARD

THE WOMEN

Nancy Wilson Ross

Essay Index Reprint Series

 BOOKS FOR LIBRARIES PRESS
FREEPORT, NEW YORK

INTERNATIONAL STANDARD BOOK NUMBER:

0-8369-1846-0

LIBRARY OF CONGRESS CATALOG CARD NUMBER:

76-117832

PRINTED IN THE UNITED STATES OF AMERICA

Contents

Such as we were we gave ourselves outright

. . . .

To the land vaguely realizing westward,

But still unstoried, artless, unenhanced,

Such as she was, such as she would become.

ROBERT FROST

We were young, we were merry, we were very, very wise,

And the door stood open at our feast,

When there passed us a woman with the West in her eyes,

And a man with his back to the East.

MARY ELIZABETH COLERIDGE

WESTWARD THE WOMEN

I. Aprons to Their Eyes

1

IT IS EASY for Americans to forget how short a journey in time they have come from the great overland trek of men, women, children, and animals which gave this country its present vast span from ocean to ocean. Actually it is just over a hundred years since the first two white women, both from the state of New York, dared the perils of that "foreign" land between the Ohio Valley and the Pacific coast to come a seven months' journey, doubled up in side-saddles — one pregnant, the other an invalid from a stillbirth — over the "impassable barrier" of the Rocky Mountains down into the green valleys of mythical Oregon.

From the beginning of the nineteenth century the shore of the Western ocean had been drawing men toward it with an inescapable pull. The pull strengthened as the century moved into the thirties, forties, and fifties. It was as though the unawakened American land, sleeping between its bindings of sea water, had itself cried: Take me, claim me, make me your own. . . . So men walked and rode, measured and staked, dug and looted, burned and planted, all the way from Maine to California, making the country theirs — some by rape and some by gentle care.

Where men go, women must of necessity follow. But that is not the whole story of the coming of the women to the West, of this long and arduous journey into deprivation and discomfort. The first to cross the Rocky Mountains came as missionaries, hoping to convert the Indians and thus to serve their Protestant God. Yet already other women had made the same journey, Indian women, serving white men, helping this alien race to conquer their own people by teaching them — the palefaces — to live in the wilderness without discontent. When the Western land yielded gold and silver, towns sprang up overnight on rich diggings, and then there came the adventuresses, the landladies and hookers of parlor house and hurdy-gurdy hall, answering a need and taking money for it in an honest and forthright fashion.

The great majority of westward-moving women, however, were the wives and mothers of the covered-wagon trains. Some of these women came, in tight-lipped protest, simply because their men had caught the virulent Oregon Fever and there was nothing to do but follow. Others were stirred with the American appetite for change, and gladly left sheltered towns and farms in Illinois, New Hampshire, Missouri, or Massachusetts to travel toward a legendary land. There were some who were sick of seeing their children and menfolk shaking their livers out with ague along some Midwestern river and so themselves organized the family exodus. "Well," cried Mrs. Waldo, for whose husband, Dan, the lovely Waldo Hills of Oregon were named, "in the spring I am going to take the children and go to Oregon, Indians or no Indians. They can't be any worse than the chills and fever."

Though eminent men of presumable knowledge — United States senators among them — decried the western migrations as the mass acts of insane people, nothing could check them once they began. No lurid tales of endless deserts, unscalable mountains, cannibal Indians, and trackless forests stopped the westward surge. For more than three decades thousands of Americans moved slowly day after day across the limitless landscape to settle eventually in struggling communities at fords or ports or clearings in the forest, or to go apart into wilderness solitude, clear a plot of land, and there erect a cabin in which to make a home and raise a family.

There are no simple explanations for the mighty forces that set a whole people in motion. The intimate, heroic, sordid, and glorious saga of the women of the covered-wagon trains moving westward will never lend itself to ready phrasing. Somewhere between the sentimentality of overblown speeches at annual Pioneer Picnics — held in high summer in most Far Western towns — and the bored indifference of the grandchildren of First Settlers lies the material of the greatest American legend:

[4]

a legend which, like all legends, is equally compounded of truth and myth.

2

It is men who have written the world histories, and in writing them they have, almost without exception, ignored women. Another cast of male mind, that of the philosopher, has seen fit to treat women as special human creatures, the possessors of traits so peculiar as to make them objects worthy of separate classifications under Man. Even the *Encyclopædia Britannica* has followed this latter tradition. Pressed in — somewhat symbolically — between Felucca, a vessel, on one hand, and Femerell, a lantern, on the other, you will find Female: "The correlative of male, the sex which performs the function of conceiving and bearing as opposed to the begetting of young." You will search in vain, however, through the M's for the "correlative" of "female."

"Women are history," said Spengler, in one of those quotable phrases which are apt to dissolve into meaninglessness if subjected to too logical a scrutiny. For he added: "Men make history," which would seem to imply that men direct women's historical course — a view in agreement with the protestations of most American feminists who argue that man has given woman complete freedom in this country and then refused to accept her use of it if it lay outside the established patterns.

The first of Spengler's aphorisms seems peculiarly apt when we study the history of the great migratory push westward on this continent. It is not possible to say or to write anything about this period in America's development without including women's role in it. For it was women who made possible the conquest and civilizing of the vast Northwestern area — beginning with Sacajawea,* the Indian guide for Lewis and Clark, and continuing down through the many nameless stout-hearted

---

* The author has used the now generally accepted popular spelling of this Indian heroine's name, although some authorities insist that it belongs to no known Indian language and that Sakakawea only is correct.

white women who held the very wilderness at bay and finally vanquished it with their insistence on larger clearings, garden patches, wooden floors, roads, schools, and club meetings.

Although the woman of the covered-wagon trains has been regularly presented in Fourth of July oratorical terms as The Pioneer Mother, she refuses to remain merely a generic term. She emerges from the Western saga in too many instances an integrated and powerful personality. Such women as Mary Walker, Eliza Spalding, Narcissa Whitman, Sister Aloysia, Abigail Duniway, and Bethenia Owens do not yield to anonymity. Many of them have left a record that will happily preserve them from such a fate.

And it is this written record — miraculously escaping destruction at the hands of timid descendants fearful of reflections on grandmother's grammar, or careless ones who cried: "Oh, burn that old thing, it's all water-stained!" — that has given us much of our information about the Far Western frontier period. Though it is said that Captain Cook's niece started the morning fire with the most valuable part of his great journal of discovery, such a record of feminine unconsciousness can be balanced by the wisdom of a few daughters of pioneers who chose to ignore their mothers' pious written requests to burn their diaries and letters immediately upon their discovery and "pray be so good as not to read them."

3

Getting to the Pacific Northwest in the early nineteenth century was an ordeal that we can scarcely imagine today. The first women to endure it were forced to travel in the rough company of fur traders, the only men who knew the trails and water holes, and the ways of buffalo and Indians. Later emigrant companies selected captains from among their own number for the plains trip and hoped somewhere to pick up expert guides to help them cross the Rocky Mountains and choose their final destination. Frequently these guides lost their way and led trusting companies into weary weeks of delay and danger when food ran out and people died of hunger and exhaustion within a few days' journey of the promised land.

Sometimes women grew desperate on the trail and set fire to their wagons, struck their children, threatened to kill themselves rather than endure another hour of heat, flies, dirt, dust, weariness, lack of water, lost cattle, sick babies, and a receding horizon. One account in a journal of the times gives a clear picture of a distraught woman who had come to the end of her endurance:

"September 15. Laid by. This morning our company moved on, except one family. The woman got mad and wouldn't budge or let the children go. He had the cattle hitched on for three hours and coaxed her to go, but she wouldn't stir. I told my husband the circumstances and he and Adam Polk and Mr. Kimball went and each one took a young one and crammed them in the wagon and the husband drove off and left her sitting. She got up, took the back track and traveled out of sight. Cut across and overtook her husband. Meantime he sent his boy back to camp after a horse he had left, and when she came up her husband said, 'Did you meet John?' 'Yes,' was the reply, 'and I picked up a stone and knocked out his brains.' Her husband went back to ascertain the truth, and while he was gone she set fire to one of the wagons that was loaded with store goods. The cover burnt off with some valuable articles. He saw the flames and came running and put it out, and then mustered up spunk enough to give her a good flogging."

Women who didn't go to these lengths in their despair frequently made what men called "trouble." "The greatest trouble was with the women who wanted to stop and wash up regularly," complained an old-timer. It is easy to understand why. So thick was the dust on the Oregon Trail that it rose like a wall in the wake of a passing company. So deep became the ruts that they can still be pointed out along the highway in many parts of the West.

A descendant of pioneers, remembering his mother's story, leaves an account that has in it all the horror of weeks of alkaline dust in hair, clothes, skin, mouth, eyes, ears — and no water, nights on end, for bathing:

"My own mother was thirteen and a half years old when she started across the plains with her parents in April, 1847, but she walked practically all the way from the Missouri River to the Willamette Valley [in western Oregon]. She was the oldest of six children, and as there were some loose horses and cattle every day which would not follow the trail unless made to do so, she was required to 'trail' behind them and see that none was lost. To be sure, the distance made would not average more than ten or twelve miles a day, but it necessitated walking in the dust caused by hundreds of tramping oxen and horses, besides the duty of keeping the stubborn or contrary or indifferent animals from lagging behind. And her duties were not deemed particularly hard when compared with those assigned to every other member of the train who was old enough to stand alone."

Some of the names of the women who endured the hardships of the westward trip with fortitude and cheerfulness have come down to us. There was an Aunt Pop, "one of the Woolery women" who relieved the growing despair of the Naches Trail party by her drolleries in the face of death by starvation. Her gaiety often followed on a brief spell of crying over their plight, and these shifts of mood enlivened the terrible monotony of that famous and almost fatal "short-cut" across the Cascade Mountains. The unfortunate emigrants who took the Naches Trail in 1853 found it nearly impassable, with bluffs so precipitous that they had to kill their cattle, dry the hides, and let the wagons down over the steep cliffs, while men, women, and children scrambled to safety as best they could.

The story is told of how Mrs. Longmire, of the same party, walking ahead in the midst of the untouched coastal forest carrying a babe and leading a three-year-old child, came suddenly upon a grizzled woodsman who blanched to the beard at sight of her and cried:

"Good God Almighty, woman, where did you come from? Is there any more of you? You can't get through this way. You'll have to turn back. There ain't a blade of grass for fifty miles."

But Mrs. Longmire simply walked past him with her face set to the west and, as she passed, said only: "We can't go back, we've got to go forward."

High-strung women exhausted themselves on the long trek with the necessity for constant watchfulness of their children.

Over and over again diaries and letters speak briefly of a child fallen into the campfire or under the wagon wheels. "All four wheels passed over his body. Small hope is held of his recovery." "Little Agness B. fell into the fire today. Poorly."

One of the famous injured children of the wagon train of '43 was Catherine Sager, whom the missionary Whitmans adopted along with her six orphaned brothers and sisters. It was Catherine who left one of the most moving accounts of the last day of the Whitmans, and of the terrible massacre in 1847 in which these famous Western forerunners and fourteen other residents of the Waiilatpu mission — including two of Catherine's brothers — lost their lives.

Blessed was the wagon train that numbered a doctor among its members. Those few doctors who traveled west — particularly during the cholera epidemics that piled up the bodies along the wheel tracks — were worked to the point of exhaustion. Women, of necessity, had to learn the practical details of nursing and bone-setting, the simple herbal and home remedies with which people relieved their miseries in the middle of the nineteenth century. One-day stopovers for the birth of a child were deemed sufficient. Time was pressing and women in labor, or weak from the birth, were expected to endure without complaint the agony of the racking motion of clumsy wagons on rough land.

When there was a death the burial was brief and furtive. Often, because of Indians, they dared not stop for days to bury a corpse. At night a fire had to be built around the "dead wagon" because the stench of decaying flesh drew the wolves from miles around. After the body was laid in the earth they drove the wagons over the spot to deceive the Indians, then pushed on. Like Mrs. Longmire in the forest, they dared not look back.

4

The western trip was not, however, always dreary and discouraging. Pleasant homely pictures of life in some of the wagon trains have come down the years. A Mrs. Van Dusen, migrating from Michigan to Oregon, had only happy memories of the journey, particularly of the cosy little kitchen in her wagon. Her recollections, as told to a contemporary, read not unlike those of a modern trailer-house enthusiast:

"On the center cross-piece was placed a little round sheet-iron stove, about the size of a three-gallon bucket, with a little tea-kettle, a boiler and frying pan. On this little stove cooking was done with great ease and satisfaction. Mrs. Van Dusen says that many times she sat in her cosy little kitchen on wheels and cleaned and cooked a bird while the wagon moved along. On cold nights their little stove made their house very comfortable. They had also a little churn in the kitchen. The milk was placed in the churn each morning and the motion of the wagon churned it, so that every evening they had fresh butter. In this way one cow furnished them with sweet milk, buttermilk, and butter daily."

There are stories of moments along the road when people relaxed and played, danced to the tune of an amateur fiddler as the big moon came up over the River Platte, or, farther west, on the hard-packed prairie with the Shining Mountains, sighted at last, ringing the skyline.

Such celebrations were frequently impromptu weddings, with perhaps a bride's cake made from turtle eggs found in some passing creek.

There was plenty of tragedy, humor, romance, and melodrama in the life of the wagon trains, but the heartache of a lifetime's separation from friends and relatives was the part of the great adventure most difficult to accept:

"From the day the little company of emigrants turned their faces toward the west in 1848, Moriah Crane never beheld kith nor kin again on earth. John Crain sent word from his distant home, 'Don't take Moriah west of the Rocky Mountains,' but her husband's mind was her mind" — and so Moriah went, among nameless hundreds.

A young bride, who was able to see how "romantic" a wagon train looked with its white canopies blooming palely at dusk beside a river under the trees, wrote some poignant phrases on a rainy evening:

" Raining tonight. Looks rather dreary to me when it storms and I cast a thought upon that quiet little home that once sheltered us from wind and rain, but it is never to be seen again perhaps by me — and again does my mind linger around those fond ones I've left, those that sleep in death, and those that surround the fireside."

In yellowed diaries, recopied by Far Western Historical Societies, curtains rise briefly on scenes of comedy or violence that must have relieved the homesickness momentarily:

"We met two of the bloomers at the river. . . . Mrs. Tait with a mind as changing as the wind has adopted the bloomer dress. . . . Two more bloomers this morning. Mrs. B. Allen and Miss Balbot. They are so tall they look very antick."

"Oh, what a wicked place. [Waiting to cross the muddy Missouri.] Swearing, fighting and drunkedness. It appears to me this afternoon as though there would be a solumn judgment sent upon this encampment before morning. . . . All kinds of wickedness going on, card playing and fighting and robbing. Last night a man was murdered by a man that he had hired to drive his cattle — his head split open — throat cut — the murderer was caught — had a trial — the officers delivered him to the emigrants — they hanged him this afternoon."

"I am quite sick with something like the lung fever. As the door was opened I see one man with a pistol in his right hand and a cowhide in the other whipping another over the head and face."

Some women learned to shoot and some did not. One woman, a Kentucky frontiersman's daughter, who was an expert in handling a rifle, was praised because she "never affected it in mannish ways." One spirited pioneer of Washington shot at the legs of a marauding Indian, filling them with buckshot. When no other Indians came to his assistance the woman dressed his wounds as best she could and made a litter in which he could be carried back to camp. Having taught him his lesson, she nursed him until he got well, and he was ever after a friend.

5

There was usually enough of threat and uncertainty in the Western adventure to keep women in a constant state of paralyzing fear: fear of hunger for themselves and their children; of disease and accidents without medical help; of their husbands killed and scalped by Indians and themselves taken prisoner as slaves. Yet in spite of all their fears the women came west by the hundreds. And having come, they stayed. Sometimes the staying seems the most remarkable part of it. "Well, we've come to the jumping-off place at last," they said when they could go no farther toward the setting sun. Often after saying it they turned away and wept, and children remembered all their lives the look on their mother's face:

"I think I can see my mother's face now, with such a discouraged expression on it. She said then that she would have sold out for a picayune."

Even when they reached their destination there was nothing for these women but harder work and increased discomfort.

"We landed at Skipanon, January 20, 1845, and camped in a hole, dug for a cellar."

"It was December . . . when the family reached the site of Ellensburg. There was nothing in sight save sage brush and dead bushes."

"As soon as possible the little cabin was finished and all twenty-four people, twelve of whom were children, moved in. Until they could build a second cabin, those twenty-four people lived peaceably in that one room."

"During father's trip he had seen two stumps standing only a few feet apart and he laughingly told mother she might live in them. . . . She insisted that father clean them out, put on a roof, and we moved in, a family of eight persons."

The giant trees from which stumps of these dimensions came were another of the sources of fear for women accustomed to the open valleys and the gentle groves of the Midwest and the East. Anyone who has dwelt close to the forests of the Pacific Northwest must have felt at times an almost primitive terror of the enclosing greenness of the trees. Children of the first settlers on the West coast remember their long tramps to school through perpetual twilight with only a rare glimpse of sky overhead. In the spring, particularly, the play of light upon the jungle luxuriance gives the sensation of drowning in moving green waters. Sometimes the effect is hypnotic and soothing, sometimes suffocating.

APRONS TO THEIR EYES

"Timber!" cried an old-timer. "Timber till you can't sleep!" He made the remark to the sharp-tongued critic George Nordhoff, who visited the West in the seventies and who was himself deeply affected by the "endless continuity" of the trees. In little isolated sawmill communities in some rude clearing on a river bank, Nordhoff said he often felt that if the mill once stopped "sawing away for dear life the forest would certainly push it into the river."

But there were many women who, in the long solitary days, never once heard the comforting hum of a busy mill, and who often found themselves alone at nightfall, their husbands away, their children too small for comfort, the forest on all sides of them and no escape except through its murky green tunnels.

And by night the forest was more baleful than by day. With the coming of darkness it seemed to push more relentlessly against the little cabin. Outside the log walls it waited, alive, breathing slowly, as though threatening to move again onto the painfully cleared square of land. Later, as night deepened, the forest spoke: cougars screamed like tortured women, wolves howled, there was the heavy tread of bear and panther, the snapping of a twig, the breaking of a bough, the mysterious whisper and the rustle. What good were wooden bolts, sharp knives, and boxes of cartridges against the primitive terror of the pathless Western forest in the dead of night?

Those late-comers among the pioneers who stopped and drove in stakes beside some welcome river in the dry inland country were no less courageous than those who braved the uncut forest farther to the west. These were the people who saw the vision of deserts in bloom, saw the time when little ditches of life-giving water could be channeled from a main stream. Yet before these barren valleys could turn green with famous orchards there were years of solitude in baking sun and freezing cold without the shelter of a single tree; a lifetime of dry winds, sand-storms, ticks, snakes, and coyotes on the endless stretch of desert with nothing to relieve its vast monotony but the whirling dervish dance of bunch-grass.

[13]

6

The night voice of the forest, and the eerie silence of the desert, were second in terror only to the noises the Indians made. In real or mock war dances, in mourning their dead, or in welcoming a change of season, the aboriginal songs and cries out of painted faces chilled the blood of white females. It is surely only in retrospect that an Astoria pioneer could write with a degree of objective calmness:

"Many Indians were camped on the hills near our house, and they seemed to keep up an incessant howling. As Sally, their queen, was very sick, they constantly made night hideous with their medicine performances. The queen's slaves were in mortal terror lest she should die and they be buried alive with her, according to tribal custom."

Even when Indians were friendly they had to be watched. They thieved without conscience, brought lice and vermin into the scrubbed cabins of white women, thrust their filthy fingers wonderingly into the mystery of rising dough, and were shameless about their nudity. The courage with which pioneer women disciplined Indian upstarts is amazing. They chased them with brooms and sticks, slapped their hands when they reached for pies, burned them by pressing stolen hot cakes against their bodies after the Indians had snatched and hidden them under their armpits. At the same time, in true feminine style, they tried to reform them, teach them Christianity, encourage them not to drink and smoke, to help their squaws with the hard labor, and to learn a sense of time and responsibility. It was uphill work, but their ardor for reform never flagged.

7

In spite of the terrors of being left alone, the women did not cling to the men, often forced to leave them to go east for reinforcements, or to act as guides over the mountain passes for family and friends; to fight Indian hostiles; to travel to some designated open spot near a spring in a forest to meet with other men and, in the American way, set up a "government by proclamation," plan schools, elect sheriffs, or fulfill jury duties in the midst of the wilderness.

Wrote the golden-haired Narcissa Whitman — she of the tragic end — to her husband, Marcus, when he went east on his controversial "ride to save Oregon": "Stay just as long as it is necessary to accomplish all your heart's desire respecting the interests of this country so dear to us both — our home."

Wrote Mrs. Lee to the missionary Jason, her husband, when he left her in Oregon, pregnant with her first child and knowing that she would bear it, during his absence, among strangers: "If you feel it your duty to go, go, for I did not marry you to hinder but to help you in your work." She had dark premonitions and fears for which she chided herself, but they proved not to be unfounded. Both she and her babe died. The news was brought to Lee as he journeyed overland, and he was able to pick up a fresh bride in the East and bring her back round the Horn, to die also in the wilderness.

Jason Lee was not as callous as this might seem to indicate. Though a missionary, he was a highly practical man. He knew what a necessity women were in conquering the wilderness, how much Western development depended on getting them there in increasing numbers. It was only unfortunate that so many women, under the rigors of this new life, died young. Little wonder the Reverend Mr. Lee wrote so wistfully of the lives of the French Canadians comfortably married to Indians well adapted to a primitive existence: "Very fortunate indeed are these happy-go-lucky voyageurs in finding such capable women to make them homes."

8

Out of all the letters and the diaries, the journals and the memoirs of and about pioneer women, a simple paragraph, concerning a female whose name was Samantha Trout, tells the story for many:

WESTWARD THE WOMEN

"Samantha Trout thought a lot about the west, and wondered how people could live. She learned they lived by their own efforts on the food they raised and by the things they fashioned with their own hands. She got along with what was in our cabin. A box nailed to a log was a cupboard. A bunk was a bed. She cooked in a fireplace. She was not lonesome. Her three children were both care and company. The furniture made of split pine sufficed. As time passed the homestead took on the air of an estate. Seasons and crops and babies filled her time and mind."

Samantha — if we may judge from this account written by her husband — was able to take everything pretty much in her stride. Not all the pioneer women were as successful. A woman on the Rogue River has left scraps of a journal from the fifties that strike a different note:

"Alone all day finish a new dress. Wish I had some new book to read to pass off time with some prophet or advantage. . . . O! dear I am tyred of the same dull monotony of time.

". . . think if I had the company of some lively female acquaintance I would feel better.

". . . I have got a pretty little pet, a yong hare but am fearful it will not eat.

"Today Oh! horrors how shall I express it, is the dreded washing day.

"O! could I see through the future if but one step.

"O! dear today I have so much to do. Mr. B is agoing to have his house raised and I have got to get diner for about twenty persons besides being bothered with two lady visitors . . . dinner is over and I am hartly glad of it for I never did like to cook."

Still there are the blessed Sundays when her "dearie" or her "honey" is home with her "alone together" and she can write: "Today is bright warm and beautiful. Honey and I are alone spending a happy day in reading, writing, and interchanging of thoughts and ideas."

And near the end of her briefly kept journal is an entry which in all likelihood accounts for the silence that then falls upon the diary of America Rollins Butler:

"I am sewing on a little dress, one of the first I ever made."

APRONS TO THEIR EYES

Some women — unlike Samantha Trout, who was entirely occupied with seasons and crops and babies — managed to keep their forebrains alive in the wilderness even in the absence of libraries and other minds equal to their own.

By the 1860's the village of Walla Walla — along with its vigilantes and its desperadoes — could boast of a Madame Bauer, a distinguished lady who spoke French, German, Spanish, and Italian, besides being a Hebrew and a Latin scholar. Though Madame Bauer gave language lessons to the officers and their families stationed at Fort Walla Walla, and was responsible for one of the first dictionaries in Volapuk — a language expected, before Esperanto, to become the universal tongue — she was also not above teaching darning, point lace, and old-fashioned cross-stitch.

Mary Richardson Walker, a missionary wife who came in the late thirties to Tshimakain, near the present city of Spokane, has left an invaluable record of a lively mind functioning in wilderness isolation. In her little dirt-roofed hut, with its makeshift doors, windows, and chimney, Mary Walker pursued at first hand her studies of minerals, plants, animals, geology, and Indian languages, while bearing six children in nine years and laboring daily an average of sixteen hours as shoemaker, tailor, carpenter, weaver, soapmaker, milkmaid, nurse, and cook.

The fact that they were supposedly the "weaker" sex spared women no labor. "Men around here would be ashamed to be seen milking a cow," one female pioneer remarked tartly. Another reported that she was the first woman to try to milk the vicious Spanish cattle in her settlement, and could only do so if her husband held the horns. Not all men were as helpful. When Father De Smet bought the Belgian nuns a goat to give them milk on their seven months' sea voyage from Antwerp to the Willamette River, he offered no lessons in milking it. Though one of the Sisters was almost washed off the deck in a high storm at milking time, all the Reverend Fathers took it calmly. Life in Oregon was to require of the gentle nuns the

[17]

highest degree of endurance and fortitude and they would be wise to prepare themselves for their trials in every possible way.

Sister Joseph of the Steilacoom nuns, who are credited with bringing to the Pacific Northwest the Scotch broom that now gilds the spring countryside, labored in true masculine style. She walked the ridgepole of the rude nunnery, nail and hammer in hand, to repair a roof; tore down single-handed in the middle of the night — when the workmen were away — a chimney they were building improperly. A woman with a critical eye, she sawed off the unpleasing head of a statue of St. Joseph and "put one more becoming to a saint in its place." Sister Joseph's father was a noted architect, says her chronicler. How much such a simple line speaks of secret frustration!

9

Though the life was hard and exacted of them the physical endurance of men, pioneer women remained in large measure reassuringly feminine. Rather than wear the same calico skirts as every "klootchman" (Indian woman) in some crude village on the coast, they would pass up the fresh bolts of cloth from round the Horn and go on turning, patching, and piecing their own worn garments from the States. These dresses, individual in color and fabric, were a slender thread holding them to their old lost life.

They tried too to save some remnants of their youth and good looks on the long western journey by hiding themselves deep in the scoop of their ugly sunbonnets. Nothing pleased them more than to be told when they reached The Dalles in Oregon that no one would believe they had just crossed the plains, because they weren't at all sunburned.

Against all rules, in secrecy and mulish stubbornness, they hid articles that they considered essential in the carefully packed wagons, where nothing worth less than a dollar a pound was supposed to be placed. Certain women won a measure of local immortality by succeeding in smuggling a wall mirror through to the coast, or little shell boxes for a Christmas celebration, or seed bags containing future flower gardens.

In spite of sharing hardships equally with their menfolk the first pioneer women managed to retain an intuitive sense of the importance of indirection in the handling of those presumed to be masters. A little story survives from the Indian Wars to illustrate how women went about getting their way. "Why should I be afraid of Indians?" asked a certain Mr. Jackson of Washington Territory, whose wife was trying to persuade him to seek the shelter of the nearest fort. "I can load this gun quicker than you can run around the cabin." "Can you, indeed!" said Mrs. J. and she challenged him to prove it. His rifle was an old muzzle-loader which required that the powder be tamped in with a piece of muslin. She got the heaviest piece of cloth she could find in the cabin, handed it to him, and shot out the door. Round and round the cabin she ran — casting in guardedly triumphant glances as she passed and repassed the single window. At last he admitted his defeat and they moved to the fort.

During these same wars women sometimes gave vent deliberately to mild forms of hysteria which released a good deal of strain and tension. A group of irritated females once presented Lieutenant Phil Sheridan, who was to become a famous general in the Civil War, with a red petticoat as a flag of dishonor and a symbol of their disapproval of the way he was conducting their particular local segment of this shapeless conflict with the Indians. Lieutenant Sheridan had trusted an Indian named Umtux, whom all the women considered a traitor. When he received the gift of the petticoat the lieutenant is reported to have flushed, then paled, before coldly replying that if it should be the good fortune of his company to be ordered to the front, this flag would be carried into action, and if so carried would be dyed a deeper red before it was seen again. When the lieutenant was proved right in his judgment of the Indian's character, the women came around to apologize. The one who had lent her petticoat wanted it back — for red flannel petticoats were beyond value — but the officer refused to yield up the garment.

WESTWARD THE WOMEN

As the pioneer era wore on, women, becoming aware of the historic role they were playing, showed signs of acting on the life around them in more direct ways than smuggling mirrors into wagons when their husbands' backs were turned, or sending red petticoats to military men of whose tactics they did not approve. Well before the turn of the century Western women were beginning, slowly but accurately, to evaluate their part in the mighty experience that lay immediately behind them. At reunions of pioneers women were rising to speak, sometimes simply and sometimes dramatically, of the important part females had played in the great Western marches.

Eva Emery Dye, a gifted Western feminist and writer, delivered a speech in Portland in the early nineties which expressed a new point of view: "Bertha, the Queen of Helvetia, accompanied her people on their Gallic march, spinning as she rode on her palfrey." To Bertha, said Mrs. Dye, one might compare the first westward-moving women who "came riding over the Rocky Mountains, Berthas on palfreys, unconscious spinners in the web and woof of history."

By the 1870's descendants of the first Western women pioneers were refusing to be shut out of men's professions. Into the open came the tight-lipped repression of many an obedient dead wife whose daughter had watched her mother's reluctant tearing up of stable roots at a man's bidding. Abigail Scott Duniway, who had walked across the plains to the Far West, remembered all too well the great courage and endurance of her mother and other women of the wagon trains. Abigail's entire life was colored by her mother's untimely death on the plains from overwork and too many children. As a consequence she was willing to dedicate herself to riding the dusty Western roads and the mighty Western rivers preaching Equal Rights to women in crossroad schoolhouses, steamboat parlors, and churches.

Bethenia Owens-Adair, the first doctor, who was almost tarred and feathered for daring to perform an autopsy on a male, was never in any doubt as to where she got the strength to endure the loneliness of life in a profession that did not "belong" to women, or the courage to make her way against all obstacles. In her memoirs — written when she was a successful physician and surgeon — she took obvious pleasure in including the life stories of simple women of her mother's day. Mrs. Owens's perseverance in the cultivation of the first Oregon flax was as symbolic for her generation as her daughter's perseverance in becoming a bona fide doctor was to the next generation. And Bethenia knew that no matter how the community might shut her out for her daring, she would never experience a loneliness or deprivation comparable to that of which her pioneer mother wrote:

"I think the most unhappy period of my life was the first year spent on Clatsop, simply for the want of something to do. I had no yarn to knit, nothing to sew, not even rags to make patches. We had very little to cook. Salmon and potatoes were our principal diet. One of my greatest needs was a cloth for a dish rag. One day Mrs. Parrish (a neighbor) gave me a sack full of rags and I never received a present before nor since that I so highly appreciated as I did those rags."

10

Just before the century's turn a book appeared in Portland, Oregon, called *Souvenir of Western Women*. It is chiefly valuable as a sign of growing awareness, boldly set forth in the foreword:

"The purpose of this book is to record women's part in working out the plan of our Western civilization; no other civilization, perhaps, bearing so conspicuously the imprint of her hand and brain. In coming to this country through all the perils, privations, and hardships of the longest journey ever made by a migratory people in search of homes, she marched side by side with man. Upon arriving here she could acquire equally with him a part of the public domain. (The first instance of its kind on record.) "

The latter point refers to the Donation Land Claim Act of 1850, by which a woman could lay claim to 320 acres, half a married couple's allotment of 640.* Granting women land led

* This law was later amended to 160 acres apiece. It expired by limitation in 1855.

inevitably to a great rush into matrimony. From this period scandalous stories survive of married "women" seen in the backwoods still playing with their dolls. The feminist Abigail Scott Duniway went so far as to refuse to accept the land to which she had a right lest posterity call her a Donation Claim Bride. (Later she saw the significance of such a law in women's slow march toward an equal status.)

The allotting of land gratis to women was not continued over an extended period. It was, however, still another indication of the fact that women in the Far West were never a liability; that they were, indeed, desperately wanted and needed. So much was this true that by the sixties enterprising Asa Mercer of Seattle was on his way east — with the blessings of respectable West coast citizens — to recruit his cargoes of New England belles and Civil War widows for the trip round the Horn, and thereby to bring the woman supply in the West somewhat nearer the demand.

"Come West and grow up with the country!" was Mercer's plea. It was a real challenge, for the West was destined to expand at a phenomenal pace. Almost too soon its future became its present. In one generation it was transformed from the Promised Land to the Last Frontier. The women who played a role in that momentous development cannot be forgotten. They gave themselves as women — with all their strength and weakness, their ingenuity and frailty — to the land of which their men had dreamed.

It was never easy, and all the bitter pain of it comes through in the simple words of a Seattle grandmother who said:

"I can't never forget when the folks landed at Alki Point. I was sorry for Mrs. Denny with her baby and the rest of the women. . . . I remember it rained awful hard that last day — and the starch got took out of their bonnets and the wind blew, and when the women got into the rowboat to go ashore they were crying every one of them, and their sunbonnets with the starch took out of them went flip flap, flip flap, as they rowed off for shore, and the last glimpse I had of them was the women standing under the trees with their wet bonnets all lopping down over their faces and their aprons to their eyes."

II. Were Females Wanted?

THE FIRST TWO white women to cross the Rocky Mountains — and thus ensure themselves undying fame in the annals of American history — were in no way alike except in their sharing of Christian zeal. They both wanted, above all things, to bring the Gospel to the benighted Indians of the Far West. One of the two who set out in 1836 on this "unheard-of" seven-months journey was Narcissa Prentiss Whitman of Amity, New York, a blonde beauty of high spirit. The other was Eliza Hart Spalding from Holland Patent, near Utica, a plain young woman of less brilliant but more steady temperament.

In order to understand how Narcissa Prentiss and Eliza Hart, two gently reared young women, were permitted by their parents to undertake their great adventure, one must know something of the religious spirit of the American 1830's. Revivalism was current and popular. There was no shame attached to rising in a respectable congregation and crying out in anguish of spirit: "What shall I do to be saved?" The problem of the conversion of the heathen was also particularly pressing at this time. During the 1820's and 1830's tracts were published and distributed which set forth in dramatically numerical terms the task of rescuing the unenlightened. It was pointed out that the world population numbered around 800,000,000. Of this number only a paltry 200,000,000 were Christians. On the shoulders and consciences of this mere handful rested, therefore, the responsibility for spreading salvation.

Both Eliza and Narcissa in their separate environments burned with a passion to serve the Lord by becoming missionaries. On the American continent itself, in that still foreign land beyond the Rocky Mountains, there were heathen Indians awaiting the Word and the Light. A Dr. Samuel Parker came riding the highways and backroads of New York State in 1834 seeking workers for the Indian cause. He fired Narcissa Prentiss with the wish to serve. She wrote to him and questioned

[23]

whether there was a place for an unmarried female in her Lord's vineyard. Dr. Parker wasn't sure. "Are females wanted?" he asked the American mission board. He had one in mind — "education good, piety conspicuous."

Piety and education were all very well, but it was decided that unattached women were not wanted as missionaries. A bona fide husband, then, was all Narcissa needed. The fulfillment of her need came suddenly in the person of Dr. Marcus Whitman, a young Christian physician of Wheeler, who was also restless to serve the Lord in distant parts. As soon as he had Narcissa's promise to be his bride, he set off with Dr. Parker to explore the lands of the Far West with a view to establishing a mission. There was, everyone felt, no time to be wasted, for had it not been pointed out by one redeemed Christian that with the proper fervor the entire world might be evangelized in twenty-five years? And, as for the Indians, they had signified their readiness for the gospel, as far back as 1831, by sending a delegation of Flatheads and Nez Percés to St. Louis in search of the white man's religion.

The story of this Indian delegation, so often repeated in Western histories, is always the same except that there still remains some difference of opinion as to the tribes from which the delegates came and what it was they were really seeking. Catholics averred that the red men were looking for "black robes," which was to say priests, while Protestants insisted that they were after "The Book of Heaven," which was, naturally, the King James version of the Bible. Whatever their immediate concrete objective, it seemed clear to all Christians that salvation should at least be made available to them.

Natural horror at the thought of the red man's dire spiritual plight was enhanced by the reproduction, in certain periodicals, of an Indian head with an artificially flattened skull. This was a style which enjoyed popularity among some Western tribes, serving to differentiate master from slave, as only free children enjoyed the distinction of such malformation in infancy. This exaggerated elongation of the skull became a symbol of dark satanic practices among the Indians and proved capable of rousing an amount and quality of impassioned missionary zeal which only Chinese lily-feet were to equal in a later generation.

When Marcus Whitman got part way on the western journey of exploration he was so convinced of Indian need and Indian ardor that he turned around and hastened back to New York State to claim his promised bride. With perhaps a better eye for showmanship than he is generally credited with he brought home, as an exhibit, two likely Indian boys who were to accompany them west on the return journey. Legend has it that he strode into church in Ithaca, New York, on a Sunday morning, followed by the two red-skinned lads. He made such a fine effect and so startled his old mother — who thought he was still far away among buffalo and Indians — that she exclaimed aloud in meeting: "Why, there's Marcus!"

Very soon after this dramatic episode Narcissa Prentiss and Marcus Whitman were married. Their wedding, in the light of events that were to come, lends itself to melancholy symbolism. Narcissa was married in black bombazine — the color and the material of mourning. All her female relatives also wore black. The entire assemblage of guests wept throughout the ceremony. Narcissa alone, dry-eyed, was able to raise her fine clear soprano (later to be employed effectively in training Indians to sing in their native gutturals stout old tunes like *Rock of Ages*) in the final song with which the wedding company parted:

> Friends, connections, happy country,
> Can I bid you all farewell,
> Can I leave you
> Far in heathen lands to dwell,
>
> . . . .
> Can I, can I, say farewell?

She could. She did. Her final act on her wedding day was to cut off a lock of her golden hair to leave with a "treasured female friend." Eleven years later the circumstances of her dramatic death were to make this lock and others historic mementos.

Narcissa would have proved good copy for roving journalists

had there been any around to cover the first overland journey of white women. The daughter of an Honorable — Judge Stephen Prentiss — she possessed, according to contemporary accounts, all the stock attributes of glamour: golden hair, a voice "sweet and musical as a chime of bells," a fine carriage — which meant in those days generous well-held bosoms — and a dynamic spirit. Friends remembered her as "symmetrically formed, very graceful in her deportment and carriage," with a "brilliant sparkling eye." She possessed, further, certain graces of manner and deportment learned at Mrs. Emma Willard's Female Seminary in Troy. All together here was a combination of qualities which was destined to bring her, en route, the flattering yet respectful attentions of rough fur trappers, some of whom had not seen a civilized white woman for twenty-five years. The famous mountain man Joe Meek, who walked across America from Oregon in 1849 to demand help for Western settlers from his cousin, President Polk, and a sleepy Congress, could still recall as an old man the first sight of her blond beauty and the effect of her golden hair on Indians as well as whites. Narcissa herself dropped hints in her journal, *A Journey across the Plains in 1836*, of the attentions of certain fur company leaders, in particular a Mr. McLeod, who made the ladies fried cakes as a treat, lent Narcissa his big horse to swim a deep river, and at the end wished to gallop on ahead into Fort Walla Walla just to bring her a muskmelon a few hours early.

And yet by one of those curious tricks of fate which so pique the historian, the man who went with the Whitmans on their memorable journey heartily disliked Narcissa. This was Henry Harmon Spalding, a rejected suitor who was destined to play a melodramatic part at the end of Narcissa's story.

Henry had been married some time before the two couples set out together on their long trip. What is more, he was happily married to a woman who, like Narcissa, had found her opportunity for missionary service through a man with a passion similar to her own. No one has ever cast any doubts on the unswerving devotion and affection of Eliza and Henry Spalding for each other. Yet the fact remains that Henry was always bitter against Narcissa, who turned him down. Before the four set out westward he went around the countryside making uncomplimentary remarks about her which eventually reached her ears. The only one to survive in authentic quotes from this period is that he "did not trust her judgment." After all, what more damning proof of lack of judgment could exist for a man of Henry's temperament than Narcissa's refusal of his suit? His illegitimate birth, and his abandonment by his mother, had created in his sensitive nature certain compensatory needs. These needs found outlet in hasty action, flamboyant speech, and a compelling desire to run the world according to his own lights.

So well known was Henry's resentful attitude toward Narcissa, and so thoroughly did Narcissa's father understand his temperament, that Judge Prentiss thought it wise to call him into his study before the two couples left for the West to plead with him to keep himself in hand. Henry made promises. He also tried to keep them. And certainly there is every reason to believe that Eliza was more than fair. Not once did she reveal to Narcissa by word or deed any hidden rancor. Knowing this, one can but feel that for all her long thin body, "coarse voice and coarse features," Eliza was completely at rest in Henry's affections. She had already had him two years to herself before Narcissa re-entered his life. As a bride she had accompanied Henry to Lane Theological Seminary in Ohio, the better to prepare herself for any missionary field to which they might be assigned.

It was Eliza who was asked to make the final decision on whether they would exchange the Osages of Missouri for the more demanding labors with the Whitmans among unknown Far Western Indians. After praying alone in her room, she emerged to say she had decided that "they should change their destiny to the Rocky Mountains." Perhaps Eliza was truly a saint. Narcissa once wrote of her: "I have always loved her and felt as if no one could speak against her."

In the spring of 1836 Marcus and Narcissa, Henry and Eliza set out together for the vast uncharted land called Oregon, carrying with them into the wilderness their complex personal relationships. The men took one of the first of the many wagons that were later to creak their patient way across the plains and up and down the tortuous grades of the American landscape. This historic wagon, brought along to relieve the women on the journey, proved something of a nuisance, to judge from an entry in Narcissa's journal: "One of the axle-trees broke today; was a little rejoiced for we were in hopes that they would leave it." It is clear that "we" could only be Eliza and Narcissa, two mildly exasperated females banding together in their secret wish against two stubborn males. But their silent team-work was of no avail. "They" reduced the wagon to a two-wheeled cart, with the extra wheels lashed to it, and pushed on.

Though the presence of women called forth a certain amount of crude gallantry from members of the Fur Caravan with which they traveled, both Narcissa and Eliza had to realize from the outset that no allowances of any kind could be made for female frailty on their long journey. There was no place for the squeamishness accepted as proper to young ladies of the period. Neither downright danger nor sickness could possibly serve them as an excuse for delays or stopovers. They had to keep up with the Fur Caravan or subject themselves to the dangers of Indian attack, slow starvation, and prolonged death on some lonely trail.

When starting out from St. Louis, fur traders were far from anxious to be saddled with missionaries and their annoying temperance pledges, seasons of prayer, and attempts at Sabbath observance. The traders and trappers were wild and godless men, and Narcissa wrote home to her parents about the dangerous influence exerted on a Christian by their cursing, drinking, and Sabbath-breaking. "The traveler bound westward," said Narcissa, "is often wounded to that degree that it requires many months if not years before he is restored to his wonted health again. It is often said that every Christian gets so that he can swear before the journey is out."

It seems likely that the presence of the Whitman party as

appendages to the Fur Caravan was tolerated only because Marcus, on his trip with Dr. Parker in 1835, had won fame among the mountain men as a doctor. When Marcus first started on the previous trip he had had the shocking experience of being rotten-egged by ruffians as a direct hint that his presence among them was not desired. Later, however, when he was able to help cholera victims — of whom there were many in the plains and river valleys of eastern central America — they changed their attitude toward him. His success with cholera patients, plus the operation he performed on the famous scout Jim Bridger, definitely established his reputation. The operation on Bridger — to remove an arrowhead which, since an Indian fight three years before, had been embedded in his back — was performed, without anesthetic, in the presence of a large audience of rough men. After this, Marcus had been in great demand to remove embedded arrowheads from Indians as well as whites. Ironically enough, the medical skills that helped the Whitmans to get to the West led later to their tragic difficulties with superstitious Indians.

Marcus had a patient the entire way in the person of Eliza, who, with a courage that excites our admiration, set out on the terrible journey as an invalid. Though but recently recovered from a stillbirth and subsequent illness, she endured, without complaint, the months of grilling travel jolting in the crude wagon, or riding miles on horseback cramped in the tortuous twist of a side-saddle; the ground her bed, her chair, and her table; her diet largely buffalo meat, fresh or dried, which did not agree with her either way and finally made her deathly ill. Eliza's daughter and namesake wrote a little family history which contains an account of a moment on that long journey in which her mother's valiant spirit flagged. She was so spent with sickness, exhaustion, and hunger that she begged the others to go on without her, pleading: "Do not put me on that horse again." She implored them to abandon her and go ahead to their great work, only being sure to let her mother in Holland Patent know that she was not sorry she had come thus far though she must die on the way. But when she saw that they would not leave her, she mounted once more and continued.

Narcissa on the whole enjoyed good health during the journey, although — like many of the women who were to follow her hazardous trail in the next thirty years — she became pregnant on the way to Oregon. Fortunately buffalo meat agreed with her — in fact, she enjoyed it. Her mention of food throughout her journal gives the reader a sense of Narcissa's vitality which perhaps no other details could. "Husband" prepares the buffalo steaks; she "could eat them every meal." She lingers with him to pick berries as a supplement to their monotonous diet. At the long journey's end, when she settled down with Eliza for a few weeks of rest and comfort — luxury even — in the Hudson's Bay Post on the Columbia River, her description of their dinners provides one of the most vivid pictures of this feudal existence in the wilderness.

John McLoughlin, the Hudson's Bay Company's factor, was an able, high-living, international host, who fed his infrequent guests in royal style. Narcissa recounted to her family the varied menus, beginning with delicious unfamiliar soups, with nameless appetizing ingredients, very unlike the homely broths of up-state New York. Roast duck was an everyday dish, as were fresh salmon, sturgeon, boiled pork or tripe — the diner to make his choice — "and at every new dish have a clean plate." Most remarkable of all there were delicious desserts — "A nice pudding or an apple pie," made with apples from the famous Vancouver apple tree grown from the seeds brought all the way from a London dinner party in the dress-suit pocket of a ship's captain who had no occasion to dress between London and the Oregon wilderness. The seeds had been handed over to the Scotch gardener at the post, who had planted them. They grew, and the apple tree still stands in the Washington town of Vancouver. After dessert, in Continental style, the high-living Hudson's Bay factor served fruit, a muskmelon or a watermelon, and lastly cheese with bread and biscuits. This sumptuous fare was ill preparation for the dietary deficiencies of the travelers' mission life at Lapwai and Waiilatpu, but it was an exciting experience for Narcissa and a most welcome relief for poor Eliza.

The early settlers of the Far West had, of necessity, to accustom themselves to strange diets. Early Oregon's "beef neither chewed the cud not parted the hoof," as pedantic Cushing Eells of the next crop of missionaries put it, thereby letting the delicate reader know that he is referring to horseflesh. Narcissa did not quail at horse meat any more than she quailed at buffalo "jerky." In the years at Waiilatpu, when the tide of immigration began to flow past the mission door of the Whitmans, the problem of feeding the weary travelers became acute, but we find Narcissa writing home with equanimity: "To supply our men and visitors we have killed and eaten ten wild horses bought of the Indians. This will make you pity us, but you had better save your pity for more worthy subjects. I do not prefer it to other meat, but can eat it very well when we have nothing else."

Not that Narcissa was always so equable. Indeed, her own journal and the journal of such an outspoken crisp-tongued female as Mary Walker of the second missionary group reveal something of her mercurial temperament. She was an impulsive, earnest, high-strung, and generally complex female, too civilized for the existence she had chosen. She was also a soul-searcher. "I find one of my most difficult studies is to know my own heart, the motive by which I am actuated from day to day." Her suggested remedy for withstanding the influence of godless men on the western journey had been praying more, "above all in secret, for if faithful there the soul is kept alive and in health." In Marcus she had found a true mate. He could help her in her struggle with her lower nature. "I have such a good place to shelter — under my husband's wings. He is so excellent. I love to confide in his judgment and act under him. He is just like mother in telling me my failings. He does it in such a way that I like to have him, for it gives me a chance to improve." Narcissa was very close to her mother and must often have longed for one of their intimate talks together. On the way west Narcissa, the bride, had written home with revealing understatement: "I think I should like to whisper in mother's ear many things I cannot write. If I could only see her in her room for one half hour. This much I can say, mother. I have one of the kindest husbands and the very best every way."

Narcissa had occasionally a happy way of turning a phrase. Once, in speaking of lingering behind the rest of the company with "husband" to talk of home and friends, she wrote with poignance: "It is then the tedious hours are sweetly decoyed away." And again, near the journey's end, at Fort Walla Walla, the first settled community they had seen in many months, Narcissa wrote in such a way of the appearance of a rooster on the doorstep that the reader sees with sudden clarity the contrast of her present life with her past:

"While at breakfast a young rooster placed himself upon the sill of the door and crowed. Now whether it was the sight of the first white woman, or out of compliment to the company, I know not, but this much for him, I was pleased with his appearance. You may think me simple for speaking of such a small circumstance. No one knows the feelings occasioned by seeing objects once familiar after a long deprivation."

With these words one looks, through the eyes of a sheltered girl from a gentle New York countryside, at her fabulous journey through an untouched land of endless plains with herds of buffalo; at snow-capped mountains, roaring rivers, and impenetrable forests; at the strange company of rough mountain men, at the ever present threat of hostile Indians and the tactless intimacies of friendly ones, at the unremitting toil and hardship of fording rivers, climbing mountains, riding every day to the point of exhaustion.

The Vancouver interlude, as guests of the Hudson's Bay Company, with its atmosphere of hospitality and its physical comforts, was of necessity to last Narcissa and Eliza a long time. Dr. McLoughlin admired the two women extravagantly for their achievement in crossing America and did not hesitate to express himself on the subject and to praise them for their "heroism." Nightly the gallant gentlemen at the fort raised their glasses high to toast the two ladies who had managed to break down fort precedent (where the wives were all Indian) to the extent of dining in mixed company. Although Eliza and Narcissa both belonged to the "tee total Society" and urged its joys and comforts on all they met, they made no converts at Vancouver and perhaps even secretly enjoyed the gallantry of the nightly gesture in their honor. When Henry — leaving Marcus inland — returned from the voyage of exploration in the upper Columbia country to take the women away, Dr. McLoughlin protested vigorously. He urged them to remain all winter and was particularly solicitous of Mrs. Whitman, then in her fifth month of pregnancy. But Narcissa, like Eliza, decided to leave, in spite of the protestation of this "very sympathetic man." The two women went on up-river, each to a wilderness home: Narcissa and Marcus to settle at Waiilatpu among the eager but treacherous Cayuses; Eliza with Henry at Lapwai, 120 miles away, among the steadier and more intelligent Nez Percés.

There is an impressive simplicity about the single-track attempt of the Protestant missionaries to make the Indian undergo a true change of heart before admitting him to the fold of the chosen. But it was this demand that, in the end, defeated the white gospel-bringers. For the poor Indians, like simple children, could not understand the missionaries' notions of sin for which eternal punishment could be anticipated. During the eleven years of their labors Narcissa wrote home: "Some among the Indians feel almost to blame us for telling them about eternal realities. One said it was good when they knew nothing but to hunt, eat, drink and sleep; now it is bad." And again: "Of late my heart yearns over them more than usual. They feel so bad, disappointed, and some of them angry, because husband tells them that none of them are Christians; that they are all of them in the broad road to destruction, and that worshipping will not save them. They try to persuade him not to talk such bad talk to them, as they say, but talk good talk, or tell some story, or history, so that they may have some Scripture names to learn. Some threaten to whip him and to destroy our crops, and for a long time their cattle were turned into our potato field every night to see if they could compel him to change his course of instruction with them."

The difference in the attitude of Protestants and Catholics toward Indian conversion was to prove one of the real seeds of bitter controversy in early missionary days in the Far West. Many of the Catholic priests were French, with the Frenchman's unpuritanical approach to matters involving emotion. They allowed the Indians to give vent to their natural feelings with bells, drums, songs, and dance in the name of "religion," practices which Protestants of English Puritan descent could not tolerate. What is more, the Protestant missionaries insisted on an inner change, a true conversion, before they would allow admission to the church. As a result there were only twenty-two Indians admitted by the missions at Lapwai and Waiilatpu during the eleven years they were established.

Eliza and Henry had chosen wisely in going to the Nez Percés, and the work they did lived on after them. Eliza established classes in weaving and knitting. Henry established grain mills, and is credited with founding the Idaho potato and sheep industries. Convinced that the old days of nomadic hunting were passing with the buffalo, and that the Indians' only hope lay in learning some rudiments of a civilized existence, he taught the Indians to till and plow and grind their corn. Supplementing her husband's practical measures, Eliza, who could paint, made a chart six feet long and two feet wide setting forth for the Indians the Christian "facts" in picture form, as a competition to the famous Catholic Ladder. This Ladder had been devised by the priests as a means of teaching the Indians a pictorial chronology of the Christian religion and, according to Protestant accounts, showed all non-Catholics "as the withered ends of the several branches of papacy falling down into infernal society and flames, as represented at the bottom." Henry wrote to the American Board about the Catholic Ladder, saying it showed Luther branching off with the Reformation on a

road unquestionably leading to hell. In the Protestant chart
that Henry planned and Eliza painted, Luther was shown hastening away from the broad road of destruction back to the
narrow road that leads to salvation. It seems likely that these
fine points of dogma and schism escaped the Indian mind, but
they undoubtedly enjoyed — in their sly and mischievous way
— the competition they could sense between the two rival religious parties.

One of the hardest crosses the white missionary women had
to bear was the knowledge that many Indians, under direct or
indirect Catholic influence, believed that a truly godly man,
a priest, would not be married. For all their devotion and labors
at their husbands' sides, they could not but realize that their
presence was a definite handicap to the spreading of the Protestant faith.

When Narcissa's first and only child, Alice Clarissa, was born
at Waiilatpu in the mud-and-log lean-to that had been hastily
built to receive her, no one would have imagined from the re-
joicing of the Indians what cruelty the Whitmans were in the
end to receive from them. The little blonde baby entranced the
Cayuses. One of the chief men, Tiloukaikt, who was to be numbered later among the plotters against them, was the most delighted of all and said — so wrote Narcissa to her far-away
parents — that the baby was to be called "Cayuse *te-mi,* or
Cayuse girl, because she was born on Cayuse land." He even
wanted to give her some land of his own, a piece of generosity
that touched Narcissa's susceptible heart.

There is something singularly poignant about the story of the
birth, brief life, and death of Alice Clarissa Whitman. In part
this is due to Narcissa's own phrases about her little daughter,
in part to the thought that had she lived, her presence might
possibly have saved the Whitmans themselves their final tragedy — for Indians became very attached to white children in
a way that is moving to read about.

When little Eliza Spalding came along, eight months after
Alice Clarissa, she too was a favorite with the Indians. Her

mother wrote telling how they would often literally snatch the baby from her arms in their eager admiration, though after this handling Eliza reported that she had often "the mortification to pick a flea or a louse" from her baby's clothes. Many years later little Eliza — grown to be a mother and even a grandmother herself — went back into Nez Percé country, and though it was long after the closing of all the Oregon missions, she met an old Indian who knew her at once, wept at sight of her, and called her by name.

Alice Clarissa was born on Narcissa's twenty-ninth birthday. The delivery was apparently an easy one, for on the second day Narcissa wrote that she sat up in bed to dress her child. She had plenty of milk and gave grateful thanks for it — for to be without milk for a child in pioneer country was indeed a tragedy. Narcissa, a little later, was to witness the painful trials in this respect of another missionary wife, Mary Walker, and even to give of her own milk for a while to Mary's hungry infant.

Alice Clarissa was a precocious little girl. At the age of one she was "beginning to talk considerably" and Narcissa wrote home to the grandparents the details she was sure they would want to know, such as the extent of Alice's vocabulary: "Papa, Mamma, Sarah, Trim, Pussy," and so on. During the school hours for the Indians, Alice Clarissa would take her own little stick and point out her A B C's. At eighteen months she was able to repeat some words of their daily hymns, and was particularly fond of the sounds of the Indian tongue that her mother had set to the old Presbyterian tunes.

"O, how many melancholy hours she has saved me, while living here alone so long, especially when her father is gone for many days together," wrote Narcissa to her beloved sister, Jane, revealing thus the loneliness she was at some pains to conceal from her family.

It is almost impossible to imagine now the solitude that these women were asked to face. Eliza Spalding was at Lapwai for an entire year before she saw a single white person other than her husband; then the monotony was only broken by the Whit-

mans, coming and bringing their babe to wait for Eliza's de·
livery. As for letters, Narcissa got none from home for two
years and five months after her departure. Getting mail was a
hazardous business. It was sent by Hudson's Bay Express across
country with the *voyageurs*, or by ship round the Horn via the
Sandwich Islands, or carried by some chance traveler crossing
the plains. Yet Narcissa wrote faithfully. It was her only con·
nection with the world she had left. In the letter in which she
spoke of her former "melancholy hours" she said: "You see,
Jane, Alice has come and laid her dirty hands on this letter,
and given it a fine mark. I send it as it is, so that you may have
some of her doings to look at and realize, perhaps, there is such
a child in existence."

In letters and diaries of the period — particularly in those of
the missionary wives of Oregon — one is impressed by the deep
responsibility that these women took for the children they felt
God had personally placed in their care. Shortly after the birth
of Eliza Spalding at Lapwai, Mrs. Spalding noted in her rather
sparsely detailed journal the receipt of a letter from Mrs. Whit·
man. In this letter Mrs. Whitman asked: "Would it not be well
for us mothers to devote a special season and unitedly present
our infant charges before the mercy seat?" Mrs. Spalding re·
plied suggesting that Narcissa name an hour which they would
together "consecrate for this exercise." They decided on nine
in the morning, and although they were one hundred and
twenty miles apart, beset with household care amounting to
hard labor, constantly intruded upon by Indians who were no
respecters of privacy, they managed to go apart daily to read
Scriptures and say prayers for their children "in unison."

This was the first step in the organization of the famous
Columbia Maternal Association, which later missionary wives
carried on after their arrival in the Far Western field, and of
which Mary Walker's detailed journal gives more information.

During the two years of Alice Clarissa's life the missionary
group in inland Oregon was reinforced by the arrival of eight
honeymooning young people from the East, also dedicated to
saving the Far Western Indians. These young missionaries

were to prove themselves reassuringly human in spite of the high dedication of their lives. It took strong-fibered dynamic people to embark on the Oregon adventure in early days, and docility was hardly their outstanding characteristic. Cramped quarters, material deprivations, exhaustion from long travel and monotonous diets, along with the inevitable friction between unlike personalities, produced trouble. Not only were there difficulties over who went with whom to which mission, and who did what when he got there, but also over more minor matters like the propriety of females praying in public, the chewing of tobacco by missionaries, the use of real or bogus wine at sacrament time.

Underlying the complicated relationships of this group — so intimately bound together by a common will to serve the Lord and by the necessities of co-operation imposed on them by life in the wilderness — there was also the still unresolved tension between Henry and Narcissa, which expressed itself in discord between Henry and Marcus. Narcissa in writing home implied that Henry's subtle poison against her was infiltrated throughout the entire mission group, acting as a slow corrosive agent. His "pretended settlement" with her father before they started west had done no good. "His principal aim has been at me; as he said: 'Bring out her character' 'Expose her character,' as though I was the vilest creature on earth. It is well known I never did anything before I left home to injure him, and I have done nothing since, and my husband is as cautious in speaking and thinking evil of him or treating him unkindly as my own dear father would be."

How could a refusal of a suit rankle so long and bitterly in the heart of a man who was as happily married as Henry? It seems psychologically sound to conclude that Henry's bitter feeling must have been due to over-sensitivity about his illegitimate birth, and perhaps some thoughtless phrase of Narcissa's — or gossip repeating some careless words — created in his mind the conviction that his rejection had somehow to do with these unhappy facts. Whatever the reasons, the discord in the Oregon missions makes sorry reading.

WERE FEMALES WANTED?

The death of Alice Clarissa for a time wiped out all ill feeling. Every missionary shared with the Whitmans their grief at the loss of their little daughter. They were never to have another, though Marcus was to ride a total of many hundreds of wild miles delivering children to more fortunate parents.

The day of Alice Clarissa's accidental death was the Sabbath. To one of Narcissa's faith this must have seemed a special grace, helping her to bear the agony of her loss. For a week before — so Narcissa wrote her parents — the child had slept out of her mother's bed, where she had remained since her birth. Of her own accord she had asked one night to sleep on a mat on the floor. "This gave me a very strange and singular feeling that she was laid away for the grave." Narcissa was deeply disturbed. She did not sleep much the first night of separation from her child and decided to make up a bed beside her own so that she could lay a hand on the little girl in the night to satisfy herself of her presence. Occasionally during that week of separation Narcissa did reach out and take the child into bed with her, but Alice always wanted to return to her own place. "Thus," wrote Narcissa, "she gradually went out of my arms . . . so that I should not feel it so severely as if torn from them at once."

On the Sunday that she was drowned, Alice resisted her morning bath — an unusual occurrence on which Narcissa was to look back with questioning pain. After family worship her father had taken her into the garden with him to look, no doubt proudly, at the fruit of his and the Indians' labors, and while in the garden he gave Alice a stalk of pieplant, of which she was very fond and which she called "apple." It was his last gift to his daughter.

Alice had been playing in and out of the open door, but when it came time for dinner and she was not around, Narcissa sent Margaret, the young Indian house-helper, to get her ready for the meal. The little Indian did not find her, but, without coming back to say so, went on into the garden for vegetables for dinner. While she was gone, Mungo, a Hawaiian servant at the mission, came into the kitchen to speak with Dr. Whitman. (Hawaii, or the Sandwich Islands as they were then called, was a near "neighbor" of early Oregon and natives of the Islands played a minor but significant role in early West coast history.) Mungo had to report the odd fact that he had seen two cups floating in the river. Marcus, intent on his Bible-reading, said only: "Let them be and get them out tomorrow because of the Sabbath." But Narcissa, passing to and fro in the kitchen about her household tasks, suddenly remembered her child taking two cups from the kitchen some time that morning. She cried out in terror. Where was Alice? Where was the Indian girl who had been sent to find her? So great was Narcissa's sudden fear that everyone ran from the house at once. Reds, whites, and half-breeds gathered for the frantic search. They ran down to the brink of the river near the place where the child was actually hidden, but "as if forbidden to approach the spot, though accessible," they passed her, crossed a bend in the river far below and then back again, and then in another direction, still farther below. Some waded into the water, looking and feeling with their hands, but strangely they all entered the river below the spot where she was at last found.

Finally an old Indian entered the stream and brought the child's body from under a root. Narcissa, in a letter to the grandparents, re-created the full horror of that tragic moment:

"I ran to grasp her to my breast, but husband outran me and took her up from the river, and in taking her into his arms and pulling her dress from her face we thought she struggled for breath, but found afterwards that it was only the effect of the atmosphere upon her after being in the water."

Narcissa made the child's shroud herself. Some chroniclers have it that she made it from her wedding dress, but the truth seems to be that it was made from the same gray dress she wore for the long journey west. Narcissa confessed to her parents that they kept the child for four days before burial. "She did not begin to change in her appearance much for the first three days. This proved to be a great comfort to me, for so long as she looked natural and was so sweet and I could caress her, I could not bear to have her out of my sight." But finally she had to be put away in her grave and Narcissa took up once more the routine burden of her crowded, empty life.

Although she had no other children of her own, six years later she wrote home to say that she was now the mother of eleven: three little half-breeds — one boy and two girls — and seven orphaned emigrant children, whose parents had died en route to Oregon. Of these the youngest was only five months — a sickly, malnourished, neglected, and dirty child whom Narcissa could not resist. "The Lord has taken our own dear child away so that we may care for the poor outcasts of the country and suffering children."

Narcissa's heart always went out to the most pitiful cases. Her little half-breed boy, whom she named David Malin after a former school-friend in the States, was brought to her in a sad condition. He was the child of a loose Indian woman and a wandering Spaniard. The mother abandoned him to the care of a filthy and greedy old grandmother who brought to Narcissa the three-year-old, covered with body and head lice, half-starved, with a bad burn on the foot where vicious Indians had pushed him into the fire, and a ragged bit of animal skin as his only garment. Narcissa tried to harden her heart against him. By this time she knew Indians, and realized that the old grandmother would in all likelihood insist that Narcissa owed her something for the favor of relinquishing the unwanted child. But Narcissa's will was not strong enough to refuse the little boy a home. She was particularly upset by the way in which older Indian boys — to shame and tease him — had cut his hair. It was shaved to a strip an inch wide from ear to ear and from forehead to neck. So she took him, "washed him, oiled and bound up his wounds and dressed him and cleaned his head of lice." The little boy became a favorite. As his fear of ill-treatment wore off he turned out to be a sweet, mild-mannered little lad, who learned English very fast. On Sundays he would walk about the room whispering to himself: "I must not work — I must not work." Soon he too was singing with all Narcissa's other charges such songs as *Lord, Teach a Little Child to Pray.*

Narcissa was a good mother to her adopted brood. She was

surprisingly modern. In a letter written home in 1846 she went so far as to outline her ideas for the care of children and ventured even to believe that she had made certain improvements on her mother's ways, particularly in the revolutionary matter of daily baths for children, which she reported seemed to do them no harm. The adults at Waiilatpu mission took to bathing daily in the river in summer, and at least once a week in a tub in the house the year round, and found this also beneficial.

The seven orphaned Sagers whom the Whitmans legally adopted — though without changing their names — had three happy years of life at the mission. From their memories of these years the Sager girls — whose brothers died on the dreadful day of the massacre — have left pictures of Mrs. Whitman which further reveal her temperament, half that of a firm disciplinarian, half that of a gay and gentle playmate: "There was no danger of any of us becoming spoiled. She would point to one of us, then point to the dishes or the broom, and we would instantly get busy with our assigned tasks. She didn't scold much, but we dreaded that accusing finger pointed at us." Narcissa was very particular about regular eating and sleeping habits. The children always went to bed after a simple supper of mush and milk. There were happy picnics, however, and each child was given a little plot of land for his own garden: "Mrs. Whitman taught us the love of flowers . . . she taught us a great deal about things of that kind and instilled in us a love of the beautiful."

Before she adopted the seven little Sagers, who, after the death of their parents, had been left to the care of other overburdened emigrants, Narcissa had consented to bring up the half-breed daughters of the mountain men Joe Meek and Jim Bridger. Bridger, it will be remembered, was the man on whom Marcus performed the operation for the embedded arrowhead on his first trip west, and Meek was the mountain man on whom Narcissa's young blond charm had registered so forcibly when she first came to the West. It was not easy to be responsible for these children of two worlds and it probably cost Narcissa many an anxious hour. When, in 1842-3, she took her first, indeed her only, long trip away from the mission during Marcus's absence on a trip east, the two little half-breed girls accompanied her. By this time Narcissa, though only in her middle thirties, was already a semi-invalid. Her eyesight, from overstrain and no glasses, had almost failed her. She had heart trouble and an internal sickness so serious that Marcus felt he should speak warningly of it to her family, and Narcissa records that she had treatments for ovarian tumor from the doctor at Fort Vancouver when she went there to visit.

Narcissa's prolonged trip away from Waiilatpu was made during the year of Marcus Whitman's controversial "ride to save Oregon," 1842-3. Marcus really went east to try to clear up mission trouble, born of tattle-tale letters sent to the board by certain carping members of the missionary group. The mission board had written peremptorily closing the Lapwai and Waiilatpu missions and suggesting that Henry Spalding come home or settle down out there, away from his mission, taking five hundred dollars for a settlement. Marcus rode east to put the true case before the board and to beg them to reconsider.

Whitman's grilling winter ride — because of the writings of some of the Oregon missionaries — has become in the minds of certain historians a patriotic journey to save the Oregon country from the clutches of the British. Henry Spalding declared that the United States was ready at the time to trade the whole vast area for a British cod-fishery. The Oregon question was a standard subject of debate in Congress, with Southern senators blocking passage of all bills to include it in the Union because they wanted it only if a slave state.

Marcus did not "save" Oregon, but he did rouse new interest in it. He spread the word that the land was habitable, that women could get there and live there — even cultivated women like his own wife — that America would be wise to lay claim to this promising country while she still could. He visited Horace Greeley, who found him, in appearance, "the roughest man we have seen in many a day," but who spread through his newspaper Whitman's word about the Promised Land. Marcus also visited the mission board and deeply embarrassed these Chris-

[43]

tian gentlemen by the outlandishness of his pioneer garments. He got to Washington and is believed to have talked with President Tyler and James Madison Porter, the Secretary of War, whose interest in a possible Oregon Trail was acute, inasmuch as it would, of necessity, lead through land that was still foreign and Indian-infested. More important than all, Whitman gave great assistance to the famous emigration of 1843 — the first sizable overland trek — by lending to its members his wise counsel and long frontier experience. He personally persuaded a number of families to embark on the journey, and may be safely credited with stimulating the flow of emigrants who, in the end, by their rapidly increasing numbers and the vociferousness of their pleas for attention, put Oregon Territory into the Union.

After his trip east the Whitman house was destined to become a way-station for weary emigrants. Narcissa and Marcus took upon themselves the burden of helping to provide necessities for the last lap of the long journey which often brought past their mission door exhausted and half-starved people on their way into the green river valleys on the coastal side of the mountains. During this time Narcissa was more and more frequently bedridden. Marcus too was beginning to show the results of years of exposure and overstrain. He too had a tumor, on the instep, occasioned by an old injury, but there is no sign that he ever spared himself because of it.

One of the deeply moving things about the record Narcissa Whitman left in her conscientious letters home, is the picture of the change gradually taking place in her from the dynamic, high-spirited, eager young woman who set out from New York in the spring of 1836 to the broken, saddened, and anxious invalid of the last of these eleven fateful years. But in many ways — in spite of the extra work — Narcissa, who loved people and who had kept her father's hospitable home filled with her young friends, enjoyed the fresh activity that the stream of emigrants brought. Remembering how often her mother had said in the past: "I wish Narcissa would not always have so much company," Narcissa once wrote home saying: "It is well for me now that I have had so much experience in waiting upon company, and I can do it when necessary without considering it a great task."

But also the arrival of the often destitute and always travel-weary people was a burden to her spirit. She found it hard sometimes to exist on the limited mission rations after a band of hungry people had descended and bought — at the lowest possible figure — the provisions they so sorely needed. Writing to other missionary friends in the late summer of 1844 Narcissa spoke of preparing for the new fall emigration and hoped that those at The Dalles — who must also share the burden — had "laid in a good stock of strength, patience and every needed grace for the siege." This emigration exceeded that of 1843 by about fifty per cent, and by 1845 the increase was three hundred per cent. The Pacific Northwest was on its way to becoming American whether Congress knew or cared.

But as the number of emigrants increased, so did the trouble with the Indians. Indians who had gone east and come back "educated" had little difficulty in pointing out to their stay-at-home brothers the threat that the white invasion was to them and to their lands. The Cayuses were a particularly arrogant and temperamental tribe. They lacked the equanimity of the superior Nez Percés, among whom the Spaldings had settled.

Threatening episodes — minor but significant — more and more affected the relationship between the Whitman mission and the tribe. While Marcus was absent on his ride to the East, Narcissa's bedroom had been forcibly entered in the night by an Indian — an occurrence which frightened her so badly that she decided to visit friends in settlements on the Columbia while her husband was gone. The Indians found her haughty, and perhaps they thought this was a sure way of humbling her. During the Whitmans' absence from the mission the mill was burned — an act of deliberate vandalism. As early as 1841 Marcus had endured, with impressive Christlike humility, a most insulting personal attack from a disgruntled Cayuse. Marcus's own words describe the scene quite graphically enough:

"He [the Indian] then took hold of my ear and pulled it and struck me on the breast ordering me to hear — as much as to say, we must let them do as they pleased. . . . When he let go I turned the other to him and he pulled that, and in this way I let him pull first one and then the other until he gave over and took my hat and threw it into the mud. I called on the Indians who were at work . . . to give it to me and I put it on my head — when he took it off again and threw it in the mud and water, of which it dipped plentifully. Once more the Indians gave it back to me and I put it on, all mud as it was, and said to him, 'Perhaps you are playing.' "

Marcus was willing, to the end, to practice the Christian virtue of non-resistance, of turning the other cheek — or ear.

For some time ugly rumors had circulated through the tribe that Dr. Whitman's medicine kit was a source of poison. The winter of 1847, with a raging measles epidemic and unusually severe weather, did little to improve Cayuse tempers or quiet their fears. In the interest of self-preservation it was finally decided to kill the Whitmans and other white adults who were wintering at Waiilatpu. After all, Indian logic found perfect justice in the murder of a medicine man who had failed to heal the sick. Marcus Whitman was not stopping the fatal spread of the measles among the Indians. The whites — with a natural immunity established in their blood — were not dying of the plague, a fact that increased the Indians' suspicion. Marcus had tried to persuade them to give up sweat baths and cold dips in the icy river — a standard cure for all their ailments — but this seemed only another instance of his treachery.

A number of descriptions have been written of the last hours of the Whitmans. The most melodramatic is that of Henry Spalding. There is a bitter irony in the fact that it was Henry — who had caused Narcissa and her family so much pain by his unforgiving nature — who in the end had to write the details of the tragedy to the stricken parents, far away in a peaceful New York town.

Just before the massacre Henry had been at Waiilatpu, bringing ten-year-old Eliza to the mission school. On this same trip he also stopped to visit the Umatilla Indians and spent the night with them, unaware of the fact that the Whitmans and many others at the mission he had just left were being murdered at this very time. He was on his way back to Waiilatpu the next day — still ignorant of what had occurred — when a Catholic priest (the neighboring Catholics were all spared in the massacre) rode out to tell him the terrible tale and to warn him that he too was being sought and must escape at once. A thick fog made it possible for the horror-stricken Henry to elude the pursuing Indians. He managed, by a combination of luck and a knowledge of the country he was traversing, to make his way back to Lapwai. But the trip took seven days, and he was freezing, starving, and sick with worry over the fate of his own family when he finally arrived.

He found his wife and the other three children safe at Lapwai. Eliza had refused to move to safety with her children since the news of the massacre was brought on Sunday. "We will rest on the Sabbath, for he that feareth the Commandment shall be rewarded," she had said. She sent some of their trusted Nez Percés to Waiilatpu in the hope of freeing little Eliza from the blood-hungry Cayuses, but they had had to return without her. It was a month before the ransom was effected and the Spaldings had their child again in their arms, in Henry's words, "too weak to stand, a mere skeleton and her mind as much impaired as her health." For little Eliza, whose knowledge of the Indian tongues surpassed that of any of the other captives left alive, had, in spite of her youth, been pressed into service as interpreter.

In reading Henry's succulent description of that bloody last day at the Whitman mission you ask yourself: How could he write this way to Narcissa's aging mother and father? And then you think: Perhaps, after all, Henry was wise to write as he did. Perhaps he really understood how it strangely eases the heart to know the full final details of a tragedy, as though the pinning of the horror to actual movements, words, rooms, faces, hours of day, and kinds of weather relates it to the familiar and thus makes it possible to bear.

Henry, dipping his pen, no doubt sweating with emotion and groaning aloud, assuredly with tears running down into his rich full beard, as he thanked God for his own escape, sat alone in a room in Tualatin Plains — far away from his own now abandoned mission — and wrote his description of the last act of the tragedy of Narcissa Prentiss Whitman, the first white woman to cross the Rockies:

"The massacre took place on the fatal 29th of November last, commencing at half past one. Fourteen persons were murdered first and last. Nine men the first day. Five men escaped from the Station, three in a most wonderful manner, one of whom was the trembling writer. . . . Forty women and children fell captives into the hands of the murderers, among them my own beloved daughter, Eliza, ten years old. Three of the captive children soon died, left without parental care. . . . The young women were dragged from the house by night and beastly treated. Three of them became wives to the murderers. . . . Eight days after the first butchery, the two families at the sawmill, twenty miles distant, were brought down and the men spared to do work for the Indians. This increased the number of captives to forty-seven, after the three children died. In various ways they were cruelly treated and compelled to cook and work late and early for the Indians. . . . The two sick men . . . beaten and cut to pieces before the eyes of the helpless children and women, their blood spilled upon the floor, and their mangled bodies lay at the door for forty-eight hours, over which the captives were compelled to pass for wood and water.

"Monday morning the doctor [Marcus, who had been out among the Indians with Spalding attending the sick during the raging measles epidemic] . . . returned to the house and was reading — several Indians as usual were in the house; one sat down by him to attract his attention by asking for medicine; another came behind him with tomahawk concealed under his blanket and with two blows in the back of the head, brought him to the floor, senseless, probably, but not lifeless; soon after Telaukaikt, a candidate for admission in our church, and who was receiving unnumbered favors every day from brother and sister Whitman, came in and took particular pains to cut and beat his face and cut his throat; but he still lingered till near night.

"As soon as the firing commenced at the different places, Mrs. Hayes ran in and assisted sister Whitman in taking the doctor from the kitchen to the sitting-room and placed him upon the settee. This was before his face was cut. His dear wife bent over him and mingled her flowing tears with his precious blood. It was all she could do.

They were her last tears. To whatever she said, he would reply, 'no' in a whisper, probably not sensible.

"John Sager [one of the seven orphans the Whitmans had adopted] was sitting by the doctor when he received the first blow, drew his pistol, but his arm was seized, the room filling with Indians, and his head was cut to pieces. He lingered till near night. Mr. Rogers, attacked at the water, escaped with a broken arm and wound in the head, and rushing into the house, shut the door. The Indians seemed to have left the house now to assist in murdering others. Mr. Kimball, with a broken arm, rushed in; both secreted themselves upstairs.

"Sister Whitman in anguish, now bending over her dying husband and now over the sick; now comforting the flying, screaming children, was passing by the window, when she received the first shot in her right breast, and fell to the floor. She immediately arose and kneeled by the settee on which lay her bleeding husband, and in humble prayer commended her soul to God and prayed for her dear children who were about to be made a second time orphans and to fall into the hands of her direct murderers. I am certain she prayed for her murderers too. She now went into the chamber with Mrs. Hayes, Miss Bewley, Catherine, and the sick children. They remained till near night.

"In the meantime the doors and windows were broken in and the Indians entered and commenced plundering, but they feared to go into the chamber. They called for sister Whitman and brother Rogers to come down and promised they should not be hurt. This promise was often repeated, and they came down. Your dear Narcissa, faint from the loss of blood, was carried on a settee to the door by brother Rogers and Miss Bewley.

"Every corner of the room was crowded with Indians having their guns ready to fire. The children had been brought down and huddled together to be shot. Eliza was one. Here they had stood for a long time surrounded by guns pointing at their breasts. She often heard the cry, 'Shall we shoot?' and her blood became cold, she says, and she fell upon the floor.

"But now the order was given, 'Do not shoot the children,' as the settee [bearing Mrs. Whitman outside for a parley] passed through the children over the bleeding, dying body of John. Fatal moment! The settee advanced about its length from the door [outside], when the guns were discharged from without and within, the powder actually burning the faces of the children. Brother Rogers raised his hand and cried, 'my God,' and fell upon his face, pierced with many balls. But he fell not alone. An equal number of the deadly weapons were leveled at the settee and o! that this discharge had been deadly. But

oh! Father of Mercy, so it seemed good in thy sight. She groaned, she
lingered. The settee was rudely upset. — Oh, what have I done? Can
the aged mother read and live? Think of Jesus in the hands of the
cruel Jews. I thought to withhold the worst facts, but then they would
go to you from other sources, and the uncertainty would be worse
than the reality. Pardon me, if I have erred.

"Frances [Sager] at the same time was dragged from the children
and shot; all three now lay upon the ground, groaning, struggling,
dying. As they groaned, the Indians beat them with their whips and
clubs, and tried to force their horses over them. Darkness dispersed
the Indians, but the groans of the dying continued till in the night.
. . . The next morning they were seen to be dead by the children.
. . . The dead bodies were not allowed to be removed till Wednesday
morning, when they were gathered together. Eliza and some of the
other girls sewed sheets around them, a large pit was dug by a Frenchman and some friendly Indians, and they were buried together, but
so slightly that when the army arrived at the station, they found that
the wolves had dug them all up, eaten their flesh, and scattered their
bones upon the plains."

And now Henry, as though afraid that it might really be too
much to bear, turned the eyes of the stricken parents to the
Bible:

" 'O God, the heathen are come into thine inheritance; thy holy
temple have they defiled. The bodies of thy servants have they given
to be meat unto the fowls of the heaven, the flesh of thy saints unto
the beasts of the earth. Their blood have they shed like water round
about Jerusalem; and there was none to bury them. Help us, O God
of our Salvation, for the Glory of thy name.'
"Some hair from the sacred head of your dearest daughter was
found by the army, I believe rolled in a piece of paper, doubtless cut
and put away by her own hand some two years ago. A lock was obtained by Dr. Wilcox of East Bloomfield, New York, which was
handed to me the other day. With great satisfaction I send it to her
deeply afflicted father and mother. Precious relic!"

A number of these relics of Narcissa survive. Joe Meek, coming to Waiilatpu to bury the body of his little girl — who was
ill at the time of the massacre and died as a consequence of
receiving no care — cut locks from the corpse of Narcissa for
her friends in the Willamette Valley. These locks are to be

found now in Western historical museums from Tacoma to Walla Walla.

The fate of little David Malin, the half-breed boy, seems the most cruel of all. When the boatloads of people, rescued after the massacre, set off down the Columbia under the guardian wing of the mighty Hudson's Bay Company — a force the Indians still respected — little David was left behind on the river bank. Mrs. Whitman, his foster-mother, was dead. There was no one who would take responsibility for him. Henry Spalding expressed the fear that he would fall into the hands of Catholic priests and all his good Protestant training would be for naught — yet he did not save him. One can think of worse fates for little David, even if Henry could not. Abandoned for the second time in his life, the Indian boy, alone in the driving rain, passes from history, "crying as though his heart were breaking."

Because of the importance in the minds of westward-moving emigrants of the Waiilatpu mission and its involuntary hosts, the Whitmans, their death and the destruction of the mission rocked the scattered Western communities as no other event could have succeeded in doing. The unprotected white settlers banded together to find the culprits, punish them, and, if necessary, fight all Indian hostiles. They also decided to send picturesque and hardy Joe Meek overland to lay their case before the government at Washington. Joe was a perfect choice for the mission: a physical giant, a shrewd buffoon, an Indian-fighter and bear-killer, and, in his rough way, very much a ladies' man. He took Washington by storm, imposed with Southern geniality on the generosity of his cousin, James K. Polk, the President, and left the capital, after a few months, as the first marshal of the newly-made Oregon Territory.

Thus, by her death, Narcissa undoubtedly hastened the claiming of the stretch of Western land called Oregon. In any study of the significant role played by women in opening the Far West to settlement, Narcissa inevitably emerges as a symbolic figure. As the first of the many women who were to perform the mystery of participation in a great mass movement beyond their will, and even beyond their consciousness, she had, of course, to pay with her blood. She is the very body of the sacrifice which life exacts for extensions of experience. Though Eliza Spalding's death was not so spectacular as Narcissa's, she too paid a price. Years of unremitting, disciplined toil brought her often to the very edge of the grave. She was constantly in frail health and subject to hemorrhages, through many of which she passed with no one to help her but ignorant Indians and her small children. History, however, accords only to the spiritually ambitious Narcissa that highest possible Christian accolade — martyrdom in the cause of the Lord.

III. *Eight on Her Honeymoon*

ALTHOUGH MARY RICHARDSON WALKER traveled west with three
other brides, in a honeymoon party of eight, she is considered
the "third woman to cross the Rockies." There is no proof that
Mary actually reached the summit and started down the western side of it before the other three women in the honeymoon
octet, but after reading her journal one somehow believes that
this must surely have been true.

To tell the story of this pioneer blue-stocking's trip from
Maine to Oregon and her life in the wilderness, we have to go
back to the war that broke out in the 1830's between two Zulu
chiefs named Dingaan and Moseltktze. These two chiefs of the
"maritime Zoolaks" were "allowed by God," as the Reverend
Mr. Eells said in Mrs. Walker's funeral oration, to go to war
and to continue at war until the Walkers of Maine, destined up
to then for missionary work in Africa, felt a call from Oregon
instead. Then, presumably breathing a sigh of relief, God put
a stop to the Zulu strife. It had served its purpose in discouraging the Walkers from going to Africa.

Mr. Eells seemed to imply that the eye that marks the sparrow's flight and fall readily marked the qualities of an angular,
keen-minded girl of East Baldwin, Maine, and recognized in
her the stuff of which Far Western pioneer females were made.
It is certainly our good fortune that Mary Walker's quick eye
and trenchant tongue were employed in comment on life in
early Oregon rather than in details of existence on the remote
coast of Africa. Like Narcissa Whitman, who immediately pre-
ceded her across the Rockies, Mary was faithful to her pen
through all hardships and vicissitudes. Unlike Narcissa's letters,
however, her diary was not written for a family far to the east,
but was intended for her eye alone. Although she left careful
instructions that it be destroyed by any stranger who chanced
upon it in the event of her sudden death, her Western descendants decided otherwise, sharing with Clifford Merrill Drury,

who made her story public, the opinion that she and her diary "belonged to history."

Mary was not so glamorous a figure as that other missionary to the Indians, Narcissa Whitman, nor so self-effacing and humble as gentle Eliza Spalding. She was sharper, plainer, keeneredged, a true product of the state of Maine. Mary was a feminist without knowing it, and certainly without admitting it. She began her diary at twenty-two, and thus we are enabled to follow for many years the course of a searching female mind of the American nineteenth century operating in a world designed exclusively for men. What is more, we are privileged to observe the unflagging activity of this mind in a Western environment so desolate and primitive that all the native ingenuity of the female was called into play to make it livable — endurable even.

While she was still a student at Maine Wesleyan, measuring herself against the world around her, she asked a professor how her papers compared with those of the men students. "Better, much better," the professor replied, and then he added with wry irony: "Aren't you ashamed of yourself, Mary?"

It is easy to believe that Mary swung regularly between the two poles of pride in herself and shame at her forwardness. She was a rare combination of introvert and extrovert, given to inner struggle and vague dreams while holding to life with a grasp that was both practical and realistic. When from a farm in East Baldwin, Maine, she first applied to the mission board for a post in a foreign land, she evaluated herself with unusual objectivity: "I have succeeded in combining the intellectual and domestic in a great[er] degree than I ever knew anyone else to attempt. . . . I am aware that I possess an aspiring mind. But I have endeavored and I hope with some success to cultivate a spirit of humility; to be willing to do something and be nothing if duty requires."

Life in Oregon was to exact from Mary a good many years of doing something and being nothing. Though she was perhaps by temperament better fitted to contend with the wilderness and the Indians than her husband, Elkanah, her place was in the home. Here on occasion, however — with joy and mental stimulation — she had a chance to display publicly her native powers. Once, when in her husband's absence she had to trade with the Indians on behalf of members of the important Wilkes Expedition, she made note in her diary that an Indian chief complimented her highly on her eloquence: "said I talked as forcibly as the men would have done and that the gentlemen would not have got the horses but for me."

But, even as Mary rode across the plains toward the Western world that was still legendary in the American mind, she had become more woman than adventurer — she was already heavy with child. "The minerals are interesting but I have to ride over most of them without picking them up. If I could only mount and dismount without help how glad I would be." She was then carrying the first of a family of eight, to whom she was to be a loving yet detached mother. The story survives and is told by a grandchild that, after her children were grown, a woman in Forest Grove, Oregon, said to her: "Mother Walker, you have raised seven sons and they are all good Christians and useful citizens, what were your methods? How did you do it?" And Mary replied: "Yes, I have raised seven sons and they are all Church members and good Christians." Then she paused and added: "But that's about all I can say for them."

Although Mary had determined at the early age of nine on the life of a missionary (the most exciting career open to women at this period), as she grew older she found herself seesawing erratically in her religious life. She longed for a final experience of "grace" that would lay to rest forever any doubts and uncertainties. To her embarrassment the Spirit saw fit to enter her forcibly at a Methodist revival. Later, to her relief, this somewhat hysterical experience "stood the test of orthodoxy" and she united with the staid Congregational Church in Baldwin. When as a grown woman and a successful schoolteacher she finally decided on a missionary career, she tried first for a post in Siam, to teach the families of missionaries — the only post open to unattached females. When the position went to someone else Mary was left in complete uncertainty about her future. She knew only that she wanted to go to foreign lands and convert the heathen, or at least to associate with those permitted by virtue of their sex or their marriage to lead lost souls to the Lord. Such a life seemed the only possible outlet for an inquiring mind, a bold spirit, and boundless energy.

Before Elkanah Walker entered her life, she had had an ardent suitor whose feelings for her, and hers for him, led to prolonged tormented heart-searchings. Could she or could she not marry an infidel, one who did not possess in her opinion "knowledge and piety"? Should she "to escape the horrors of perpetual celibacy settle down with the vulgar"? It seems likely that, in the end, Mary would have done just this had not some shrewd maneuvering on the part of friends of both sent to her Elkanah Walker, a pious young man from Bangor who wanted also to be a missionary but did not want to set off wifeless to foreign lands.

Elkanah came to East Baldwin to look over Mary as a prospective bride. In two days they were engaged. Afterwards, with the passing of time, judging from their letters and Mary's diary, they really fell in love. But not before Mary had had many painful and disturbing scenes with the mysterious "G." of her diary, whose presence seemed able always to shake her faith. And G. was not inclined to spare her feelings: "I would rather have seen you pass on a bier than in a chaise with W," he told her. He added: "He does not love you as well as I do." He tried to sting her by letting her know that people did not think she was "cutting any great cheese" in taking Elkanah.

Mary's own family did not make it easy for her either. Her brothers, after one look at the gangling six-foot-four frame of Elkanah, went about making the awkward noises and gawky gestures of a lapwing they had recently captured.

Finally, however, the tortured girl brought her whole struggle into focus: "I would not as I value my soul, connect myself with a bold blasphemous infidel. I feel that however strong may be my inclination to love G., it would be sinful for me to do so. I feel too that however little I may feel inclined to love

W., it is my duty to do so. I have gone so far that I cannot go back without forfeiting my Christian character."

After this the God-inspired Zulu chiefs set up their petty strife, and Elkanah Walker changed his prospective mission field from Africa to Oregon. Mary announced the news of her marriage and imminent departure, occasioning such tart Maine comment as: "Now isn't that just like Mary Richardson to go galloping off across the plains on a wild buffalo." Perhaps this remark came from the same source which set village gossip buzzing about her some years before when, as a guest in a house, Mary scandalously sat down on the floor on a skin stretched before the kitchen fire. Impulsive Mary was often shocking people. She frequently made Elkanah uneasy. On their way up the Mississippi the bride made note of a resolve: "Tomorrow I will not if I can possibly avoid it, do anything that will displease my dear. I wish he would try to make me at ease instead of embarrassing me by continual watchfulness. . . ." And later: "If I stir, it is forwardness; if I am still, it is inactivity. . . . I am almost certain that more is expected of me than can be had of one woman."

And much later from Oregon: "I am almost in despair and without hope of his ever being pleased or satisfied with [me]. I do not know what course to pursue. I can never, with all my care, make myself what he would like me to be."

Similar entries are sprinkled generously throughout Mary's revealing private journal. Her anxiety to establish a steady and adult relationship with her husband is one of the qualities that endear her to history, particularly her revealing statements about life with a moody man whom, she sometimes felt, she could never really know or be close to:*

"Husband very much out of tune. Scarce spoke pleasant all day."
"I met with an impatient unfeeling moroseness enough to reach the heart of the most insensible."

* Elkanah Walker's western descendants excuse his temperament on the ground that he suffered from a chronic stomach complaint which would today be diagnosed as ulcers.

As a wife of some years Mary made a desperately sincere entry in her faithful journal, obviously addressed to Elkanah, whom she suspected of reading her secret jottings:

"I find it in vain to expect my journal will escape your eyes and indeed why should I wish to have it. Certainly my mind knows no sweeter solace than the privilege of unburdening itself to you. It frequently happens that when I think of much that I wish to say to you, you are either so much fatigued, so drowsy or so busy that I find no convenient opportunity, till what I would have said is forgotten. I have therefore determined to address my journal to you. I shall at all times address you with the unrestrained freedom of a fond and confiding wife. When therefore you have leisure and inclination to know my heart, you may here find it ready for converse."

But all these entries lay on the other side of the great journey.

Before Mary Richardson set out for the "riddlings of Creation" she crowded into her life all the experiences possible in the civilized world of the East. In going to Oregon she was, after all, facing no less of an ordeal and no shorter a journey than had it been Africa that claimed her. All that people knew about the Oregon country in those days was blood-chilling. In congressional debates on the Oregon Question, those senators who were opposed to admitting this wild country beyond the Rockies turned many a fearful and flowery phrase about cannibalism, wild beasts, endless deserts, impassable mountains, and unfordable rivers. "The whole country is the most irreclaimable barren waste known to mankind except the desert of Sahara. As to healthfulness the ravages of malaria defy all history to furnish a parallel." This was a typical statement. The story of the overland trip of Lewis and Clark, spurred on by Thomas Jefferson and led by an Indian squaw, had never been published, and few people were aware of its significance.

Both the Walkers had mild qualms, though Elkanah, who had once experienced the horrors of seasickness on a short coastal excursion, was relieved to feel that the hazards of water travel were at least not to be theirs. As for Mary, her appetite for experience kept her days too crowded for misgivings. She visited and was feted in Boston and New York. She took her first ride on a railroad train — at some ten miles an hour. She rode to the end of the line at Chambersburg in Pennsylvania and there took stage to Pittsburgh — this last a tedious journey enduring from Thursday to Monday morning. From Pittsburgh she and Elkanah went down the Ohio River, stopping at Wheeling, Marietta, and Cincinnati.

In Cincinnati they called on the famous divine Dr. Lyman Beecher, head of the Lane Theological Seminary, father of the great evangelist Henry Ward Beecher and the illustrious Harriet Beecher Stowe, whose *Uncle Tom's Cabin* was later to rock a nation. In Cincinnati, also, Mary's path crossed that of the most daring and outspoken feminist of her time. This was Fanny Wright, who was then on a tour speaking publicly in support of her shocking theories on equal rights for women, birth control, a more equable distribution of property, and marriage as a moral rather than a legal obligation. Mary reported in her journal that Dr. Beecher was replying to Miss Wright in chapel on the subject of "infidelity."

We could wish that Mary had defied Elkanah and gone alone to see Frances Wright, who in 1818 had abandoned the life of luxury to which she had been born in Scotland in order to embrace the freedom of the New World. In her lifetime Fanny Wright was to give herself to many causes, including Robert Owens's socialist Utopia at New Harmony, Indiana. She devised a plan for the freeing of Negro slaves by purchasing them, placing them in a community in Tennessee, teaching them independence and useful trades, and eventually colonizing them in Haiti. Fanny Wright was too far ahead of her time to influence it lastingly, but she, like Mary, stands as a prototype of an emerging female. The two should have met.

We are safe, however, in assuming that Elkanah would not have approved of a woman of Frances Wright's caliber, since he did not even approve of women praying aloud in the presence of men. There was, indeed, a little storm later in the Whitman mission over this very point. Mary, waiting at the mission during Elkanah's first exploring trip away, prayed aloud in public as both Mrs. Whitman and Mrs. Spalding were accustomed to doing. She then immediately noted in her diary: "I wish I knew whether my husband likes to have me pray before folks or not. When he comes home I will ask him." Elkanah was not of two minds about it. His answer was a positive no, in which he enjoyed the backing of no less an authority than the Apostle Paul, who, without mincing words, had set it forth in First Corinthians: "Let the women keep silence in the churches; for it is not permitted unto them to speak." Mrs. Whitman remarked (with some spleen) in a letter home that men of the missionary reinforcement "found it wrong and unseemly for a woman to pray where there are men." She found the distinction insulting — St. Paul or no St. Paul.

By the time they reached Cincinnati, Mary and Elkanah had joined forces with two of the other honeymooning couples who were also dedicating their newly-joined lives to the cause of Indian conversion in the Far West. Knowing what lay ahead of them in the company of the blasphemous men of the Fur Caravan, they put to the Reverend Dr. Beecher the solemn question of their observance of the Sabbath. Dr. Beecher undoubtedly startled them, and perhaps even shocked them a little, by the eminently sane — though faintly flippant — attitude he took on the matter. Said the great divine, if he were crossing the ocean he would certainly not consider jumping overboard on the seventh day in order to avoid the onus of Sunday travel.

This was probably the kind of reply that appealed in her heart to Mary, of whom Elkanah in his intermittent journal has this to say: "It is a grief to me that Mrs. W. is disposed to read so much that is not devotional in the Sabbath. I fear that her view of the correctness of this day is very limited." And in two separate Oregon entries we find Mary breathlessly recording — just before the stroke of midnight on Saturday: "washed children and floors, cut hair and sewed," and again, "cut hair, cleaned house, etc. Got through in time to escape what I so often get, a lecture on Sabbath breaking."

Myra Eells, another bride among the famous group of eight honeymooners, left an entry in her plains diary which sets forth the spiritual dilemma that the question of Sabbath traveling proved to be to the scripturally exact missionaries: "Our Sabbaths have always been the hardest day's work. This has led me very much to question the duty of going to the heathen in this way. I cannot tell how it is consistent for us to break one of God's positive commands to keep another."

The man who was ostensibly the leader of this group of missionary recruits to the Far West was W. H. Gray, who went out with the Whitmans in 1836 and immediately made a hot-foot trip back to the States for reinforcements. He represented the Indians as panting for salvation and he managed to recruit, within a few whirlwind months, three honeymooners and a single man, besides getting a wife for himself.

The town of Independence, Missouri, was the last civilized stop for the four couples. Here they made all arrangements for the journey, including the very important matter of tent-sharing. Not without what Mary called a "mighty big fuss," it was finally settled that the Eells and the Grays would share a tent at night, and the Smiths and the Walkers another, each tent divided in half by a curtain. Thus for months by a flickering tallow, with Elkanah beside her urging her to put out the light, and the Smiths "sleeping loudly" on the other side, Mary made her faithful entries.

From the outset it was plain that there was going to be trouble. "We have a strange company of missionaries," wrote Mary in her outspoken way. "Scarcely one who is not intolerable on some account."

W. H. Gray, who published in 1870 a two-volume *History of Oregon*, shared Mary's views — excepting himself, of course. In his *History* he managed to insert not a few sharp licks at his fellow workers in the vineyard of the Lord. He didn't trouble to analyze the women — they were just women — but he found Cushing Eells guilty of a "superabundance of self-esteem, great pretensions to precision and accurateness of statement and strictness of conduct." In Gray's opinion, he lacked "all the qualities requisite for a successful Indian missionary." He found Smith a man of "strong prejudices" who was without Christian forbearance. Walker was "faithful as a Christian" but "inefficient as a preacher," with "no positive traits of mind."

What positive traits of mind Elkanah lacked, his wife more than made up for. She and the positive-minded — one might even say the bossy — Mr. Gray might have made a team. Mary has left an account of the killing and eating of a calf on the trip which gives an all too human picture of the pettiness to which exhausted and temperamentally unsuited people can descend when forced to spend day after day in one another's company.

A wolf had killed a suckling calf which belonged among the cattle the missionaries were taking west with them. Elkanah — without consulting his associates, and acting on Smith's suggestion — dressed the calf for food. Gray, probably because he considered himself the leader of the group and had not been consulted, refused to eat any of the meat. The Eells, as tent-sharers, took the Grays' side. Then the Smiths wouldn't eat. It was thus four against four and stalemate. Smith and Gray had apparently seized upon the dead calf as a symbol of their relative authority. Exasperated, Mary seized her pen and wrote about Smith in her journal: "I think S. is stubborn and have about as lief things would go on and our family devour the whole calf."

However, she refused to cook the meat until Smith and Gray settled their differences. For two days, with all the strain of daily packing and unpacking, fire-making, standing guard at night over the cattle, walking, riding, the two sulky men refused to make up. Finally a "treaty of peace was negotiated" in the Eells and Gray tent and Mary at last cooked the veal. Smith, however, was not quite able to let go of his pique. "Mr. Smith short as pie crust," wrote Mary in her pithy style.

This is the same Mr. Smith with whom Joe Meek, the genial mountain man, had an adventure of which he left an account in his biography, *River of the West*. Meek came upon Mr. and Mrs. Smith separated from the other missionaries (perhaps another little difference of opinion?) not far from the fur trappers' Rocky Mountain rendezvous at which Meek had first seen them. He found the couple all alone in the midst of a vast, hot, and dusty plain, the woman still on her feet, with the two horses, but Mr. Smith prostrate on the ground and sure that he was dying. Joe, not without malice, one feels certain, offered the missionary the succor of his bottle of alcohol. It was righteously refused. When Joe saw that the stubborn man might really die if he continued to lie on the earth in the sun, he made — so he reported to Mrs. Victor, his biographer — the following speech:

"You're a . . . pretty fellow to be lying on the ground here, lolling your tongue out of your mouth and trying to die. Die, if you want to, you're of no account and will never be missed. Here's your wife, who you keep standing here in the hot sun; why don't she die? She's got more pluck than a white-livered chap like you."

Having delivered himself of these remarks without any apparent effect on the prostrate man, Meek then informed him that hostile Indians were riding hard on their trail. Finally, in desperation, he lifted the terrified Mrs. Smith to her saddle and ordered her to ride. She rode. "Mrs. Smith can find plenty of better men than you," was Meek's parting shot. This final threat struck home. When he looked back from down the trail, Joe saw the dying man sitting up, and that night he rode into camp. After this experience it is not surprising to learn that Smith wrote back to the American Board saying that the more he thought about it, the more improper it seemed to him for females to travel across the plains.

It is not unlikely that the females had moments of doubting not alone the propriety, but the sanity of their undertaking. Even stout-hearted Mary broke down and had some good "bawls." Once, during a flood, when even the bedding was soaked, she was found weeping on a pile of it. On being questioned as to her grief, she replied that she was thinking how comfortable her father's hogs were. On another occasion she made note: "Rode twenty-five miles without alighting. Had a long bawl. Husband spoke so cross I could scarcely bear it." This was hardly the high-spirited young woman who had written while in New York: "Think I have been rather off my guard, quite too cheerful, have not been as careful as ought to maintain a prayerful spirit." Doleful airs were proper to Christian young women in the 1830's.

As Mary has let us know, Elkanah expected a good deal of his wife, and his scanty journal recorded both his censure and his approval. The items of approval increased with the passing of the years, a heartening sign of a true relationship. Mary herself has unconsciously shown that at times there did exist between these two dissimilar temperaments real understanding and freedom of expression. How otherwise could such easy lines fall from her pen to Elkanah as these? — written after they were in Oregon, on one of his trips away from her:

"I suppose you will expect a letter whether I have anything worth writing about or not. If I could converse with my lips instead of my pen (& writing the word *lips* puts me in mind what I would do with them before I commenced talking) . . ."

In spite of chronic hypochondria there were emotional depths in the reserved Elkanah, revealed most plainly in a letter that has survived from courtship days. This letter has a warm and forthright tone, gratifying to find in a period in which cold and guarded understatement was the vogue:

"I love you therefore I want you. If I could be with you this moment a more heartfelt kiss you never had than I would bestow. To fold you in my arms, hear from your faithful lips that I am still your dearest one would be sweet, sweet indeed."

There was, however, very little opportunity, time, or mood for tenderness in the long honeymoon trek across America. Everyone was expected to make the fullest sacrifice of his personal comfort and personal wishes. If the missionaries sometimes failed in Christian acceptance, it is not easy to blame them.

Mary survived better than most because she had a robust constitution and resources of the mind and spirit. She had long been accustomed to writing poetry in periods of emotional stress and undoubtedly found that she could compose well enough in a side-saddle if she gave her mind to it. She was also so interested in botany and mineralogy that the trip could never be so dull for her as it was to others: "How much the way is shortened by the company of plants and minerals," she wrote. And again, sighing perhaps as she wrote: "I wish Mr. W. would feel as much interest in viewing the works of nature as I do. I think the journey would be much less wearisome for him."

Mary had a good eye for the scenery and was particularly enchanted — as all Western travelers have always been — by the architectural fancies of the American dry lands. "The bluffs resemble statuary, castles, forts . . . as if Nature, tired of waiting the advance of civilization, had erected her own temples." When they encamped on the plains near Independence Rock, Mary chipped a piece from it and then wrote one of the first descriptions of this great landmark. It was this rock in the "dry sea" that was later to become a register on which hundreds of weary immigrants paused to scrawl their names — thereby revealing a single act of self-assertion after weeks of the exhausting, dusty anonymity of the overland trail. The piece Mary chipped from the rock may now be seen in the Oregon Historical Society in Portland, along with the little antique sidesaddle in which she rode so many cramped and tortuous miles.

After the long monotony of the dry sea there came the perilous mountains. The men of the caravan from St. Louis were expected to turn over their missionary charges to Hudson's Bay employees at a stipulated mountain rendezvous. But the Hudson's Bay men were not notified of the correct place and as a consequence the missionaries almost lost their next set of guides — which would have been a real disaster. Fortunately, according to Mary, someone had left a message on the wall of an empty cabin that brought the Hudson's Bay men through on the double. "Come to Popeasie" (Popo Agie — the place of rendezvous) , "Plenty of whisky and white women."

Looking at the relative spaces on a map, it would seem that once having reached the rendezvous for trappers and traders in the Rocky Mountains, the journey for the honeymooners was nearly over. Actually, however, the greatest dangers still lay before them. They had yet to cross the Continental Divide, "the backbone of American scenery," as Myra Eells, another bride, spoke of it in her journal. The perils of mountain horseback riding were by no means insignificant.

"You know I am not skittish at all," Mary wrote home after a descent "steeper than the roof of a building commonly is," "but I could scarcely sit my horse." She must have looked back with amusement on the timidity she had felt in crossing by bus, far back on the journey, the Tuscarora Mountains near Chambersburg. During those days of hard mountain riding Elkanah lost his wedding coat, a loss so sorrowful that Mary italicized it in her journal. He also gave his watch such a severe jolting that she was sure it would have to go to England for repairs. Myra Eells wrote that the ladies all lost their veils — a notation that gives us a picture of their attempts in the high altitude to protect themselves against the ravages of insects and the burning sun.

When, finally, they reached the Whitman mission at Waiilatpu, their trials were still not at an end. Living-quarters were woefully inadequate. Mary had no chance for the privacy for which she, as an expectant mother, now longed. She wrote to Elkanah, away on a scouting trip looking for a site for their own mission, that she dreaded the coming of cold weather, when she could not stay in her unheated room any longer and must beg a place beside Mrs. Whitman's stove.

Surely one of the hardest of all the pioneer trials was the fact that they were never safe from the prying eyes of the Indians. The Indian was curious and he saw no reason to restrain his curiosity. He was always there, appearing suddenly and silently, in the doorway, at the window, inside the room itself, gazing in mockery or wonderment, following like a shadow which could never be lost — ill-smelling, lice-ridden, flea-bearing, and red-skinned.

"I scarcely do anything from morning till night," wrote Mary later from their mission, "without being seen by some of them. Sometimes I feel . . . I cannot endure it any longer, and then I think if I do not teach them in this way, I never shall in any way. [Yet] I suspect that many of them never think of trying to imitate the things they see me do anymore than we should think of imitating a play actor whom we had been witnessing."

The Walkers and the Eells chose to settle together among the Spokanes (also known as Flatheads) in the idyllic little valley called Tshimakain, named by the Indians for a spring that bubbled there. Mary's description of the untouched countryside which was to be her home for nine years — and perhaps in a sense forever her spiritual home — manages to convey the unawakened quality of a land where man has not yet intruded:

> This is a beautiful country,
> Still a kind of gloom seems to pervade it
> As if Nature were asleep,
> Or rather the face of the ground.
> The whole country might be supposed to be
> Enjoying a long Sabbath.

It was here that Cyrus, the Walkers' first-born, was taken shortly after his birth at the Whitman mission, where Mary had remained until her confinement. She was not sorry to leave the Whitman household for a place of her own, though it was only a fourteen-foot-square log hut with a grass and dirt roof (which leaked mud in every rain) , a dirt floor with pine needles strewn on it, and the skins of animals tacked at windows and doors.

There was a persistent undercurrent of strain and bad feeling among the missionary wives when around Narcissa Whitman. Indeed, through Mary's sharp yet essentially kindly eyes, we get another view of the martyred Narcissa's high-strung emotional temperament. We see her not eating her breakfast, going down by the river to have a good cry; spending long hours in prayer alone, coming impulsively afterwards to ask forgiveness for her faults; "in a worry about something; cross with everyone"; so that she "went out and blustered around and succeeded in melting over her tallow." Yet Mary also saw the other side of the matter; that the presence of so many strangers was a burden to Mrs. Whitman, and that she had "less help from the other ladies than she ought."

Mary's delivery, for a first child, was not a difficult one. Her phrases about it, written in immediate retrospect, have a rather dry humor: "About nine I became sick enough; began to feel discouraged, felt as if I almost wished I had never been married. But there was no retreating; meet it I must." After the delivery she endured a kind of suffering of which one can hardly bear to read. She had, according to Mrs. Whitman, "no nipples." She undoubtedly had milk fever. To nurse her child was an agony so terrible that she says herself Elkanah had to hold her and the babe too: "The pain I experienced was so intense that my hands would be clinched and a paroxysm produced much like a fit. I think I can say with truth that I never knew what pain was until then." But little Cyrus had to be fed, and there was only one cow at the mission, going dry. Mrs. Whitman helped for a while, then an Indian woman was found. It must have been strange indeed for Mary Richardson Walker of Maine to see her first-born nursed by one of the heathen people she had come to save.

In spite of this terrible post-birth experience Mary went right ahead and had her other children with courageous spirit and few complaints. Sometimes the doctor got there and sometimes not. Once Mary met him at the door with her babe in her arms. The courage of these missionary wives in their childbirth experiences never ceases to amaze a modern reader; partly because all of them were old for childbirth by nineteenth-century standards. They were in their late twenties or thirties. Poor Myra Eells, who was always sickly, was thirty-six at the birth of her son, Edwin, and we read of a Mrs. Hill who was so ill with a disease of the spine that she could not ride horseback or sit upright in a canoe and yet she produced a child.

It is good to read stout-hearted Mary's strong and simple phrasing on the days of her delivery:

"Rested well last night; awoke about four a.m. Rose at five, helped about milking, but by the time I had done that, found it necessary to call my husband and soon the Dr. Had scarcely time to dress and comb my hair. Before eight was delivered of a fine daughter."

EIGHT ON HER HONEYMOON

And again:

"Rose about five. Had early breakfast. Got my house work done about nine. Baked six loaves of bread. Made a kettle of mush and have now a suet pudding and beef boiling. My girl [Indian] has ironed and I have managed to put my clothes away and set my house in order. May the merciful be with me through the unexpected scene. Nine o'clock p.m. was delivered of another son."

Even when the little flock was beginning to spring up around her skirts in mushroom style, Mary continued to keep up her journal. "I find my children occupy much of my time; that if their maker should see fit to withhold from me any more till they require less of my time and attention, I think I should be reconciled to such an allottment." Since Mary did not capitalize the word maker we are free to speculate whether she referred to God or Elkanah.

In spite of the drudgery of her life she made time for the little extras that give a child pleasure. She wrote about sitting up late to make a "rag baby" for little Abigail and then not being able to resist going to the child's bed and waking her to see her look of joy. She worried for fear she might force the children too fast for their natural development and warned herself by recalling an impatient childish habit of hers of picking open the buds of roses to hasten their blooming. Her detachment on the whole seems admirable. She wrote once of an altercation between Elkanah and little Cyrus in which the child refused to yield an inch. He was put to bed as punishment, but when Mary tiptoed in to look at him she was pleased to observe: "He has gone to sleep with a smile of exultation depicted on his countenance. I hope if he is ever called to suffer at the stake, he will be as unrelenting."

There was a good deal of heart-burning among the missionary mothers incident to the question of how, in the midst of an amoral race, to bring up children after the good American Puritan pattern. Poor Mary had an Indian girl "helper" who was dismissed by the whites and condemned by the Indians for

[69]

"asking young fellows to sleep with her," as Elkanah expressed it. While Elkanah was away on a trip, Mary rehired the girl to help her with the washing, but the pious Mr. Eells counter-manded the order, sending Mary to her diary with Scriptural complexities beyond her own unraveling: "I do not know what is right. I have compared her case with the example of our Saviour in the case of the woman taken in adultery, and of the woman of Samaria, and of his eating with publicans and sin-ners. Also what St. Paul says of keeping company with im-moral persons. I cannot determine exactly how we should treat the present case or whether Paul would have us not to pay any regard in our worldly transactions as to whether they are moral or not. . . ." There spoke the true Yankee realist who knew that the world's work must go on — washings must be done re-gardless of the private sins of the laundress.

The missionary wives of the reinforcement became members of the Columbia Maternal Association, which Narcissa Whit-man and Eliza Spalding had established the first year they were in the West. Each mother spent the anniversary of the birth of each child in fasting and prayer with the charge whom she felt God had personally placed in her care. The rules of the Maternal organization contained, among subjects for dis-cussion by the women at their rare meetings together, the fol-lowing: "The importance of the aid and cooperation of our husbands in training our children in the way they should go." These pioneer women had almost as difficult a time as modern ones in interesting their work-tired men in the problems of a growing family. Certainly Mary had to handle her children single-handed. Elkanah was much away, trying to wrest a liv-ing from the wilderness, learning the Indian tongue, and teach-ing them the white religion and civilized habits. This necessi-tated going with them to their fishing-grounds and on their hunting and root-gathering expeditions.

Though there were long days of solitude for Mary in the lonely countryside, there was, always, endless work to be done. Just to read the chores enumerated in her wilderness journal makes the back ache. Her work day averaged sixteen hours.

EIGHT ON HER HONEYMOON

Sixteen hours of washing, ironing, sewing, mending, painting, carpentering, baking, repairing roofs and chimneys, helping the invalid Mrs. Eells ("cleaned Mrs. E's earthen ware. Cooked for both families") milking six cows night and morning, making soap and butter. Even cheese-making was added when the ingenious Mary at last hit on the use of a deer's rennet in place of the calves' rennet which she could not get. She also made all the family's garments and their shoes: "cut out eight pairs of shoes." She salted beef, cleaned tripe, wove carpets, churned, tried tallow, dipped candles: "sat up all night . . . dipped twenty-four dozen " — and all this labor was accomplished without even the primitive equipment that at the time passed for conveniences among more favored American women. But somehow one cannot pity a woman who can write (after she has lived for some time with a dirt floor) : "Find it pleasant to have a floor to wash again," even though she could also remark: "Sometimes I wish there was a way to live easier." Perhaps this note of discouragement crept in on one of the occasions when a newborn infant was proving "very tendful."

Mary was accustomed to sit up late, either working or reading. Her lively mind allowed her no rest. Although, in order to help her husband with his work among the Indians, she had to learn the Spokane language, she frequently chided herself for making so little progress in the translation of hymns into the Indian tongue. This was a difficult task, as the sounds the Spokanes made in speech were like nothing so much as the sounds of husking corn. Mary had to teach the Indians white ways by constant precept and example and also give them some knowledge of the world outside by direct educational means; thus she set out to teach them geography with the aid of eggshells painted to represent the globe. She kept up a correspondence, as a part of her obligation to the Columbia Maternal Association, with a Maternal Association in Capo Palmas, Africa. (The other missionary wives also reached out from their wilderness hide-aways to remote parts of the world: Mrs. Smith wrote to Constantinople, Mrs. Gray to "Singapoor," Mrs. Eells to Holden, Massachusetts, and Mrs. Spalding to Prattsburg.)

In Cincinnati, on their way west, when they were buying necessities for their wilderness life, Mary's journal had noted: "Think I shall prevail at last in having a botany, geology and mineralogy." She made good use of this limited library. When, as a joyful interruption to her months of solitude, men of learning came to the little hidden valley of Tshimakain she had something to share with them besides domestic chit-chat. Indeed, she was so impatient with time-wasting when there were fresh minds to tap that she commented tartly on Mr. Eells's monopoly of the conversation during the great Peter Skene Ogden's visit: "We had a very pleasant visit, except there was too much trifling conversation and Bro. E's. ego was quite prominent. When a man of such extensive information is present I regret to have the time occupied with trifles." Probably Mary was not at all sorry that both husbands were away when members of the Wilkes Expedition, surveying the still unclaimed west for a rather indifferent United States government, came to spend the night. She sat up after midnight talking and has left a picture of herself offering a "stirrup cup" of milk on their departure. These were the men for whom she bargained with the old Indian chief, winning his praise for her handling of the situation. She reported also that one of the men "took a specimen of the soda and several minerals that I happened to have."

A wandering botanist came through and we find Mary writing: "Spent most of the day arranging dried plants. Find my collection is becoming large." An artist named Kane also came along, and although she called him "an ungodly man of not much learning," she noted that "he gave me considerable information about birds." Another artist visited also, John Mix Stanley, who painted Elkanah and little Abigail — portraits still in existence. All in all, it is surprising how many signatures Mary collected for the combination autograph and guest book that she kept in her lonely log house.

But surely the most touching section in Mary's diary is her account of experiences in taxidermy, an occupation which fills a number of entries in the year 1847:

"August 1847 Tues. Purchased a bow and a trout and salmon skin and spent half the afternoon stuffing and fixing them.

"Wed 4. Bought a mocking bird.

"Thurs 5. Stuffed a sparrow skin and bought a rattlesnake skin ready stuffed, except that it wanted fixing a little nicer. . . .

"Fri 6. Purchased a duck skin and stuffed it, also a cross bill. Mr. W. gets out of sorts not liking my new trade of stuffing birds, etc.

"Tues. 10. Purchased a few stuffed skins but think I will wait until I can procure arsenic before I collect more.

"Wed 18. Bought four partridges.

"Sat 21. In the afternoon skinned and stuffed a small bird.

"Wed 25. Spent the afternoon in skinning a crane; think I will not undertake another crane soon."

Although entries indicate that Elkanah did not share Mary's enthusiasm, he did at least allow her to proceed: "Got permission to continue collecting objects in natural history." For once we feel that Elkanah may have been at times a sorely tried man. He must have found it difficult to understand why a woman surrounded on every side by wild life should persist in her effort to bring it dead into her crowded house. Perhaps, however, this was one way of establishing a subtle dominance over the all-powerful world of nature on which man here had made so little impression.

It was John Mix Stanley, the painter whose visit Mary had so greatly enjoyed, who sent the letter that was to alter the course of the Walkers' lives. He dispatched his Indian guide, Solomon, to report the terrible massacre at the Whitman mission. This meant that the Walkers and the Eells and their children would have to leave the gentle green valley that had been their home and go to some place where there would be protection from hostile Indians. Though their own Indians were friendly and grieved to have them leave — feeling that by this act on the part of the missionaries they, the Spokanes, lost face as protectors — there was nothing to do but follow the advice of the military men.

Mary wrote a poem for her children to keep as a remembrance of their birthplace. It reads the way an old sampler looks:

[73]

Tshimakain! Oh, how fine, fruits and flowers abounding,
And the breeze, through the trees, life and health conferring.
And the rill, near the hill, with its sparkling water
Lowing herds and prancing steed round it used to gather.
And the Sabbath was so quiet and the log house chapel
Where the Indians used to gather in their robes and blankets.
Now it stands, alas! forsaken: no one with the Bible
Comes to teach the tawny *skailu** of *Kai-kó-len-só-tin*.†
Other spots on earth may be to other hearts as dear;
But not to me; the reason why, it was the place that bore me.

Even in the dark days that followed their departure from the home in the valley she had learned to love, Mary was true to character. In walking around Fort Colville, where they had gone to await further orders from the Army or the mission board, Mary regarded the scene with her usual observant and analytical eyes: "Took a long walk by the river. The stone stratified. I should think felsparic rock. Very nice for building, very brittle."

They could not go back to Tshimakain. The future was shapeless and uncertain. All the whites were under a fresh burden of fear, not knowing what the Indians were plotting. Yet, wrote Mary, in a phrase of simple strength: "I am afraid to fear."

When finally they left for the valley of the Willamette with a "rescue party," she made the most of this new trip. One of the guides, writing an account of the journey for the *Oregon Spectator,* particularly mentioned Mary:

"Passed the day quite agreeably in the company of Madam Walker, conversing on the natural history of the region, character of the natives, their manners and customs, volcanic eruptions, tertiary or igneous or aqueous geological formations. 'An intelligent and virtuous woman, her price is above rubies.'"

Not long after leaving Tshimakain, Mary and Elkanah took up their residence in a typical Willamette Valley community, Forest Grove. Mary's journal has less to record from this time on, and there are also fewer letters. She took her place in the

* *skailu* — people.   † *Kai-kó-len-só-tin* — God.

more prosaic existence of a Western village as her children grew up and went out into the world.

The slow tempo of her life was quickened once by a trip to Maine on the early railroad. Here she was pointed out as a curiosity, the first local woman to ride across the plains. (In all probability the buffalo myth had gathered weight with the passing of the years.) Mary enjoyed herself enormously on this journey and exhibited her usual independence of spirit by junketing off alone, without Elkanah, to visit relatives. This upset and exasperated him and finally brought him to her.

Mary is said, by a descendant, to have once signed a letter: "Your loving but not always obedient wife." When in 1877 Elkanah, on his deathbed, tried to extract from her a promise never to remarry, she refused on principle, although she certainly had no intention of marrying again. She did, indeed, mourn her husband deeply and confided to her journal with characteristic simple expressiveness: "I feel so lonely. Think of so many things I want to tell Mr. Walker. I realize more and more how much more I loved him than anyone else

And now I recollect with pain
The many times I grieved him sore,
Oh if he would but come again
I think I'd vex him so no more."

Mary lived on for twenty years. In her latter years her mind failed. From this period comes the story of the hours she would spend in the old side-saddle, placed on a chair, rocking, with her traveling cape about her, dreaming perhaps of the young bride who was one of the first to see, in all their untouched freshness and beauty the green valleys, the far-stretching plains, the varied streams, and unscaled snowcaps of the American continent.

Why the strong mind of so remarkable a woman should abruptly fade in its force and clarity is an interesting speculation. Perhaps it is not too fanciful to find the answer in the pages of Mary's diary. Here was a woman of the liveliest intelligence; a human creature so interested in the world around her that she could not find time enough in a sixteen-hour waking day to satisfy her curiosity about rocks, birds, flowers, trees, animals, vegetables, minerals, fish, Indians, human beings, God, the Bible, her children. There were not many minds comparable to her own in a pioneer society — or, for that matter, in any society. What happens when you cannot find other minds with which to share your questions and your findings? Must not the over-ardent seeker in time turn in loneliness and feed upon himself, finding elsewhere neither stimulus nor response equal to his own?

If Narcissa Whitman's sacrifice in going to the Indians was that of the body — a blood sacrifice — Mary Walker's sacrifice was surely that of the mind. Her appetite for knowledge and for the tools of knowledge — books, scientific instruments, exchange of thought — was forever unappeased. Narcissa gave her life, Mary gave her mind, to the great experiment that made it possible for white women by the thousands to follow after them, daring the solitude and the deprivations of pioneer life.

IV. One Dare Not Be Nervous in Oregon

"ONE DARE NOT be nervous in Oregon," wrote Sister Mary Loyola in her precise convent-bred hand, trying not to form the letters carelessly in her haste, though time was pressing. She had just learned that an English vessel was sailing from the mouth of the Columbia River and the letter could be carried round the Horn to far-distant Belgium and be delivered, with good sailing luck, to the Mother Superior at Namur not more than seven months hence.

"Especially in the woods," Loyola added, and, warming to her theme, proceeded to describe just what she meant. The Sisters often met wolves and mountain lions in broad daylight. Snakes lurked everywhere, even in the vegetable garden among the melons and cucumbers they had planted so prayerfully against the enfolding wilderness. Already Sister Aloysia, in her more sprightly style with its touch of wry humor, had written to Namur about the "concerts" they enjoyed at the time of high flood the preceding winter; concerts consisting of the "hissing of serpents, the roaring of the mountain lions, and the howling of wolves." Yes, Sister Loyola felt that she was justified in boasting just a little to the Mother Superior. In Oregon, said she, the nuns took the killing of snakes and the chasing of wild cattle as calmly as their sheltered Belgian sisters would brush aside a fly. Only that very morning, indeed, they had had to drive away no fewer than eight wild horses.

Sister Loyola was writing from the mission house of St. Paul's on the Willamette River on the 14th of October in 1845, nine years after the Whitmans settled at Waiilatpu. More than two years had passed since she and five other Belgian nuns had set sail from Antwerp on their long journey to the untamed shores of the great Pacific Ocean to bring enlightenment to the "children of the forest."

As she wrote her dutiful letter home, Loyola's mind's eye no doubt saw again the gentle streets of the old town of Namur, the cobbled courts and the ivied walls. She saw, too, the leafy trees, nicely spaced for the play of the wind and able each to cast its own shadow, not pressed in upon one another and upon the feeble dwellings like a breathing evergreen wall, as they were here in Oregon. And Loyola must have thought of the clean order within the Belgian convent walls, the prescribed round of tasks which did not demand such constant ingenuity and unflagging grace as their duties on the Willamette, where Indian children must be healed of scrofula, lice, and fleas; taught prayers, penmanship, needlework, morals, and good manners, all at once, all against time.

And, coming near the end of the letter, Loyola's mind went out in retrospect across the great stretch of waters on which the packet containing this letter and samples of their "orphans'" penmanship would toss and roll for more than half a year. She still remembered vividly, though twenty-four months had passed, the terrible trials and perils of their seven months' journey round South America to the fearful bar of the Columbia River. She shivered as she wrote the words: "rocky coast of Patagonia," "the mouth of the Columbia." Then as though to cheer herself she recalled the characteristic gaiety of dear Sister Aloysia on this perilous trip, and decided to write the Mother Superior what it was Aloysia said at the time of the great hurricane which so terrified the Reverend Fathers who were their shipmates: "For my part," said Aloysia, "I was seized with terror, but the calm of resignation to the holy will of God soon succeeded. I offered up my life and then went peacefully to bed. 'Ah, dearest Lord!' said I, 'if I die tonight I shall have to appear before you in night-gown and cap.'"

Hardly were the words on paper before Loyola wondered if they were not perhaps a little too flippant for the Mother Superior to read aloud to the other Sisters. To erase was impossible, to throw away the letter — crammed as it was with necessary information about their new life — was unthinkable. "A strange reflection indeed this was," Loyola hastened to add, "but it proved that the dear Sister looked on death without fear."

For that matter, each member of the little band of six nuns had been asked to look upon death without fear. Scarcely a page of their chatty letters, published in Brussels in 1847, can be read without finding some example of quiet endurance, of almost gay insouciance in the face of unaccustomed peril.

The names of the six intrepid Sisters ring a pleasant little tune in the head: Aloysia, Loyola, and Albine, Catherine, Cornelia, and Norbertine. When they started out, there were seven, but Sister Reine, during an unfortunate thirty-day becalming that they endured at the outset in the Scheldt, had the shocking experience of overhearing the language of a "disaffected Fleming" sailor. She alone among the Sisters understood his peculiar dialect, and his words had so dreadful an effect on her that she "fell into a melancholy and lost heart in her glorious enterprise," so that at Ostend Mother Constantine came to pick her up and take her back to the *maison mère*.

The remaining six sternly put from them all thought of return to their mother country or of reunion with loved ones this side of heaven, and set sail from Antwerp with resolute spirit. Within a few hours the first of their trials was hard upon them: seasickness. Aloysia's phrases for it make it all very clear:

"We left the table one after another as if we had been stricken by a sudden blow, and felt our way like little children learning to walk, clinging to chairs, or as best we could to the shoulders of those who were less sick than we. It took us some time to reach the door and then to climb the stairs, where we went on deck to pay our respects to Neptune."

And ahead of them stretched seven months of voyage by water! For seven months in high wind and treacherous calm the Sisters moved about their limited deck space in the full-skirted, modest, and bulky garments of their Order. There were dreary and dangerous weeks during which food and water gave out, rats ate their luggage, terrifying storms descended on them. There were, however, bracing days of breeze and sun, and gentle evenings when their litany floated over the waves in sight of the aurora borealis or the stars of Magellan. A gigantic flaming meteor dropped into the ocean near by to render them speechless with awe. Icebergs, mountain-high, floated past them with silent menace. And there was one dreadful night in particular, when a "brooding sense of terror" was felt by all on board because they were being followed by a suspicious-looking craft that even the captain feared was manned by pirates.

The priests who had assumed responsibility for the nuns on their long journey — notably Father De Smet, the widely traveled Western missionary — exhorted the Sisters to pray for deliverance from this dark peril. "But," reported Aloysia, the staunch, "we were perfectly calm for we had the firm conviction that we were under the protection of God and on that very day had made a promise to St. Joseph, the conditions of which we were to fulfill on reaching Valparaiso."

A favorable wind sprang up, allowing them to escape. St. Joseph had accepted their promises to honor him in Valparaiso. Mary, their patron saint, having fortunately a special relation to the ocean, bearing among her many titles that of Our Queen, the Foamy Ocean Star, also frequently obliged on the voyage with respect to breezes.

Yet the great storm off Patagonia, responsible for Aloysia's quip about her nightdress and the Lord, was, from all accounts, a fearful hurricane. The Reverend Fathers remained on deck all night in prayer, expecting the end at any moment. Of the excessive fears of the priests, Sister Aloysia had written rather pertly to Mother Constantine: "Sister Mary Cornelia, who is reputed to be the most timid of our band, said as soon as Father De Smet had left us [he had come to ask them to prepare to meet their Maker], 'I believe the Reverend Fathers are easily alarmed. Really the rolling of the vessel is not any worse than it has heretofore been!' "

Aloysia had a trick of turning a phrase in such a way that she revealed more than the words considered singly and without the weight of implication could ever in themselves convey. Reading her letters one feels that this gifted woman — who had begged as a special dispensation the privilege of making the great sacrifice of the Oregon journey, though she could ill be spared from the home convent — found the Reverend Fathers sometimes faintly annoying. In describing how Father De Smet took the opportunity during a calm off the South American coast to warn them solemnly of the dangers they would meet in crossing the bar of the Columbia, Aloysia's comment is given in a tone of patient tolerance: "We understood," wrote she, "that his intention was to inspire us with courage and resignation."

But really! one can imagine Aloysia saying to herself, why doesn't he allow us to enjoy the trip while we can? For Aloysia had a prodigious appetite for life. She was a keen observer, finding the giant sharks which actually menaced their small boat "superb creatures," remarking that certain fierce battles between porpoises and great sea birds "afforded them no little amusement." She had also a fine fancy about tropical fish. In comparison to European fish — which she remembered as quiet, peaceable, and graceful — she found the "denizens of the deep" in the tropics "ludicrous" in the extreme: "Some seem to be all tail, others all head, and some have the head where one would expect the tail to be." She wasted no false sentiment on the fish which the sailors styled "old women," because as soon as one was stabbed with a fishing spear all the others precipitated themselves upon the same "murderous steel. . . . The shoal that we saw caught in this way served as a delicious treat for dinner for several days."

By the time they were well out to sea, food had become a matter of real concern. Before they had even left the Channel the long delay of becalming had reduced their food supplies. The odor of decomposed flesh penetrated the vessel, and very early all the meat and fish had to be thrown overboard. Even the live fowl had died in the hold. Bread was unknown the entire trip and the hard biscuits came to the table with the marks of rats' teeth in them. But then, for that matter, the rats stole the food on the dining-table itself, scampering fearlessly across it at meal time. To their stolen fare the rats had also added wood from one of the side support beams of the vessel, which the captain found gnawed to the thickness of a sheet of paper when the vessel put in at Valparaiso. Here, in this South American port, no fewer than fourteen hundred rats were killed during the fumigation.

The Sisters possessed a goat, purchased for them in The Netherlands by Father De Smet after he had observed that drinking the *café noir* was distasteful to some of them. None of the Sisters had ever milked before, but they set out to learn in the readiness of will with which they approached all new experiences; one would hold the horns, another would steady the bucket, a third would attempt to draw the milk. No record is left of any of the Fathers coming to their assistance, though once during a storm the gentle milker almost lost her life, for a great wave picked her up and dashed her to the railing, where a sailor was able to catch her in time. It is not difficult to imagine Father De Smet nodding his head in approval as the Sisters struggled with their goat, for he knew from experience — where they could only envisage — the hardships and the labor that they were to face in the Far Western wilderness.

But if they had qualms and fears, the Sisters did not admit them to one another. They enjoyed everything that came their way, particularly the ceremonies with which crossing the Equator was attended, and sent home a detailed account of the experience, beginning with the cries of the sailors toward seven in the evening on the 14th of February: "The Fire of Neptune! The Fire of Neptune!" Hastening to the deck with all the speed that their garments and their dignity would allow, the Sisters beheld on the water about a hundred feet from the vessel a column of smoke. The sailors had set fire to a cask of dried peas and tar and thrown it overboard as the beginning of the few hours of homely sport allowed them on their long grim voyage.

As the excited nuns looked toward the burning cask a stern voice spoke from the topmast saying: "Captain, have you any passengers aboard?"

The captain, a hearty man in the last stages of consumption, who was making — though he did not know it, but perhaps surmised — his last trip to sea, answered merrily: "I have twelve."

"Do they intend to pass the line?"

"Yes."

ONE DARE NOT BE NERVOUS IN OREGON

"Well, tomorrow Neptune in person will administer baptism, which must be experienced by all who pass the line."

At ten that same night as they crossed the equatorial line a flame burned from the topmast, and at ten the next morning a cry sounded throughout the ship: "Neptune! Neptune!" The reverend clergy were invited to join the captain on the bridge for the ceremony, but the Sisters remained discreetly below, looking up at Neptune in his great wig and coarse flax beard, carrying a huge wooden compass and sextant, with which he pantomimed the captain taking longitude. Beside him was his "wife," and attending them both, their guard, bearing wooden swords, tridents, and spears, their faces smeared with tar and presenting to the nuns' eyes a most "hideous aspect." Neptune demanded that the reverend clergy yield to being shaved by him. There was nothing to do but submit, which each reluctant priest did in turn, after which "baptism" was administered — a deluge of water from on high that thoroughly wet them all.

When the vessel arrived at Valparaiso the good nuns of Picpus welcomed the Sisters of Notre Dame during their brief visit with such hearty hospitality that Aloysia, for one, admitted to being "somewhat confused by the assiduous attention." In Lima, also, where they stopped while the captain tried in vain to get some information on how best to cross the Columbia River bar, they were again overpowered with hospitality. They were "obliged," reported Aloysia, "to accept the urgent invitation of Señora Rivodera to visit her hacienda." More than this, "several ladies visited us and prevented us from carrying out our resolution of spending some days in silence and prayer."

The attentive ladies, however, came bearing gifts of fruit: dates, pillas, chilimoya, and pignas. The nuns were to think longingly of this fruit in the weeks to come, when contrary winds kept them at sea until the last ham was eaten, although "in such a state of decomposition that the odor was insupportable," and their supply of water was almost gone. The Sisters decided then that prayers must surely have ceased for them back home in Belgium. "Our Sisters believe that we are already in Oregon, while we are battling with an angry sea."

But at last, on the 29th of July, they came to the high point of their trip. They were faced with the necessity of somehow crossing the bar of the Columbia River, that "dreaded bar, the terror of all travelers to Oregon," which so fiercely guarded on the sea side the approach to a green and gentle country. "A dense fog hung over the mouth of the river whose waters were dashing in uncontrolled fury into the surging sea. Enormous breakers lashed themselves into foam the whole length of the bar, and as we gazed upon them from our storm-beaten vessel with its tattered sails and broken masts, the thought uppermost in our minds was, 'Will she be able to make her way?'" It seemed unlikely. The Sisters were in anguish, and toward evening, when it was apparent that, for that day at least, the crossing was impossible, Sister Loyola went to Father De Smet and said that the Sisters could always go back to Lima, where their services also were badly needed.

The next day passed in saying Masses, praying, fingering rosaries. One occurrence gave them hope. They saw a two-masted vessel which seemed to them a good omen, for they had expected to find a three-masted warship guarding the bar, having heard that the territory was now disputed ground between America and England. Two bars suggested the iconography of St. Ignatius Loyola, whose feast day was the 31st. This appeared to the Sisters a clear indication that the saint would see them over the bar on his day. And so he did — but they made history in the doing, for the good ship *Infatigable* entered by the wrong branch of the treacherous river, allowing the Sisters and priests to demonstrate a miracle at the outset of their work in Oregon.

Aloysia sent a graphic description to Belgium of the terrifying experience of two men lashed to the sides of the vessel, taking soundings and crying out the fathoms at regular intervals and with ominously lessening numbers: *"Six brasses . . . Cinq brasses . . . Quatre brasses."* At the chilling cry: *"Trois brasses,"* the captain exclaimed aloud: "We are now between life and death." It was then that the mate announced that they had taken the wrong channel. There were two and this was the one which no ship could possibly navigate. This fatal news rallied the captain. With the bravado of one who knows himself doomed anyway, he cried out: *"Bah! Vous voyez bien que l'*Infatigable *passe partout. Avancez!"*

They advanced. A few minutes later they found themselves miraculously in quiet waters. Awe-struck Indians, who had been looking on, rending their garments ceremoniously at what they took to be a scene of death, came crowding around in canoes with gifts of salmon and potatoes. The few whites hastened also to welcome them. They were invited to dine with the Governor of Astoria, Captain Birnie, his high-spirited half-Indian wife, and their seven beautiful daughters. The Sisters ate their first native berry pie — a dish which they pronounced *délicieuse.* But with what was surely sincere regret, since they had no Puritan bias against it, they refused wine with their meal, for, wrote Aloysia to the Mother Superior, they had already learned that in America, *"une femme qu'en boit se déshonore."*

From Astoria they went on up-river to Fort Vancouver, where they again enjoyed expansive hospitality, this time with the famous host Dr. John McLoughlin, the genial factor of the Hudson's Bay Company, who, dwelling in feudal splendor with his Indian wife and half-breed children, had so astonished the Whitmans. From McLoughlin's the Sisters departed in small boats up the Willamette River to their future home. They camped at night on the shore and ate their supper camp-style around a glowing fire, doing just what people have always done along the waterways and trails of the Far American Northwest. The Sisters, by now thoroughly unwound from the tensions of their long voyage, carried on among themselves as gaily as schoolgirls:

"Although we had but the ground for table and our heels for chairs, our appetites were not in the least impaired. Supper being finished Bishop Blanchet said the evening prayer aloud, to which the whole camp responded. We then sang the Litany of the Blessed Virgin and withdrew to our improvised canvas convent. As it was not yet nine o'clock we profited of the interim to laugh to our hearts' content."

And who of the six was the drollest, and who laughed the loudest? Although it is Aloysia writing, one feels certain that it was she who had them all in stitches. The mere glimpses of the nuns which the few letters from or about them afford are tantalizing. Of Mary Cornelia we know only that she "led by love, triumphed by tenderness." We see her, when they have arrived at their mission, hard at work "trying to find the floor of the church under the crust of dirt that covers it." Of Loyola, their Superior, aside from her matter-of-fact informative letters, we learn that she was considered "more than a woman" and that she could "toil terribly." Mary Catherine referred to herself as a *bouche-trou*, which is to say a jack-of-all trades. Her great accomplishment was a rare ability to do sums, since she had enjoyed the privilege in her youth of sharing a tutor with her brothers. At the mission, however, she took charge of the laundry and was regularly seen "alone for the washing in the shade of a venerable oak." Sister Norbertine won the Oregon trip for herself, in part, because she had "evinced a capacity for agriculture in the garden at Ghent." Sister Mary Albine "possessed a taste for needlework." Her deft fingers, accustomed to the finest Belgian embroidery, were to be employed hence-forth in teaching Indian women how to make the simplest, coarsest, and most modest of garments.

None of the nuns was spared the hardest toil. In their letters home they are forever carpentering, painting, glazing, gardening, mending, sewing, milking, forming bucket brigades to water their vegetables, teaching the sign of the cross and the Our Father six days a week, and studying Chinook and English in their spare time.

They were often hard put to it to keep the children interested in performing small necessary tasks around the school and church. Loyola reported home a successful device of hers for getting wood carried:

"We are now," said she to her little charges, "going on a pilgrimage and will start out by singing a canticle. When we reach the end of the inclosure, we shall each take an armful of wood and carry it to the house." The Indian children, who always loved an occasion for singing, were eager to play this new game. The first pilgrimage from wood-pile to shed was in honor of God the Father, the second was in honor of God the Son, the third in honor of God the Holy Ghost. "The pilgrimage had so much attraction for them that when the bell rang for lunch they were not satisfied until I promised them that we would afterwards make others in honor of the Blessed Virgin and St. Joseph."

The years in which the Sisters lived their busy and idyllic life on the shores of the gentle Willamette are known now as "ante-pioneer" days. These were the days before the prairie schooners. The settlers of Oregon were still, for the most part, French Canadians, retired Hudson's Bay employees. Their home spot, French Prairie, was the immediate settlement that the Catholic Sisters (and Brothers a few miles distant) were serving. Here the Canadian French "on the beautiful prairie, and in the absence of their countrywomen, had espoused the dusky maidens of the Calapooias, who raised for them bright-eyed groups of half-breed boys and girls." Even old-timers, writing years ago, thought of these days as a "quiet, peaceful, faraway life."

Though these were ante-pioneer days the Sisters found a church already built when they arrived at St. Paul's: "not a bad resemblance to the stable at Bethlehem." It had been erected in 1836 by pious French-Canadian settlers, two years before the first priests took up residence among them. The Methodists had been in the Willamette Valley before the Catholics, but they had disbanded and gone away, leaving behind them their college, mills, farms, and houses. In the interior other Protestants — among whom were the famous martyred Whitmans — were earnestly trying, in Catholic opinion, to "pervert," not to convert, the Indians. But these missionaries seemed too far away to be a real threat. For a few years nothing was to disturb the gentle busy routine of the Sisters' lives.

Loyola wrote the Mother a description of the church they found ready for them. It sagged, she confessed, rather markedly, "owing to the total absence of nails." It was furnished with rough benches, without paint or backs. A piece of common cotton cloth, fastened with four pins, decorated the front of the altar, and on the walls were only "four common prints with groupings of sixteen or twenty saints on each, pious if not artistic." But it was not long before the bustling Sisters were able to astonish good Bishop Blanchet with the transformation they wrought, first by thoroughly cleaning the church, then by bringing forth from their boxes treasures to adorn it, and finally by looting the surrounding forests for "graceful festoons, trailing vines and wild blossoms."

The Sisters had brought colored pictures from Belgium to distribute to the parishioners and pupils, but they never had enough. The Indians, it seemed, were almost fanatically eager to learn about this religion. Women and children came with scant provisions for themselves — though always with gifts of fruit, vegetables, melons, potatoes, eggs, and butter for the nuns — and slept all night in the woods so as to gain time for instruction. A poor woman was discovered to have gone without food for two days, a dog having carried off her meager supply; but she had said nothing, fearing that to return to the Indian camp would mean that she would lose her lesson in the catechism.

To give instruction was far from simple. Sister Mary Cornelia had to prepare an old Indian woman of eighty for her first Communion, and though the Sister had almost "infinite patience," the outcome seemed doubtful. Even the old woman herself remarked: "Look at my wrinkled face, look at my withered forehead, nothing can enter therein."

Yet any Indian, young or old, male or female, would weep over a statue of the Infant Jesus; and the story of the Crucifixion, the sight of the Crucifix itself, always brought ready tears to their eyes. Sometimes their misinformation on Biblical subjects was shocking in the extreme. Sister Albine presented a workman, at his request, with a colored picture as pay for a day's work. She made what she considered to be a full explanation of its theme — it was the Crucifixion — but when the Indian continued to study it with great concentration, she inquired if there was anything further he wished to know.

"'Who is this?' he asked, pointing to St. Mary Magdalene. Sister Albine briefly related to him the story of Mary Magdalene. 'I have heard of her already,' he said. 'But I always thought she was the Blessed Virgin's sister. And did our Lord have any brothers?' "

What did Albine reply? How did she explain the Magdalene, how make clear to the simple Indian his gross error about the two Marys? Aloysia, reporting it, does not say. She remarks only: "Sister was very glad of the opportunity to give him the desired information, and he left for home perfectly satisfied, and happy in the possession of his picture."

The Indians entered with zest into all forms and ceremonies. The pupils at the school hastened to avail themselves of the novel experience of Confession, "although they can hardly be understood, and it is necessary to have them repeat two or three times before the meaning of what they say can be grasped." Feast days and holidays were regularly celebrated. The nuns adhered to all the festivals of European boarding schools. At the Epiphany the children drew for the coveted roles of the Three Kings and, wrote Aloysia, "we decorated them with all the finery we could lay hands on." They even had a marriage ceremony, following hard on the baptism of a sixteen-year-old Indian girl who married "good old Baptiste," the mission factotum, who made himself useful baking bread, salting meat, gathering fuel, tending the farm.

The celebration of Sister Loyola's "patronal feast" was a great occasion. Premiums were distributed and entertainment provided, the "central feature" of which was a "conversation, or dialogue, on the Creation of the World, the Fall of Our First Parents, and the Redemption." This piece of religious theater, in the grace and dignity with which the little Indians and halfbreeds performed their parts, far surpassed Loyola's expectations. After the dialogue the Sisters presented Loyola with a frame for the colored picture of the Holy Family in Egypt already given her by Father De Smet, and this presentation allowed Loyola to compare their lot here on the Willamette with that of the holy three in Egypt:

"Like Mary and Joseph we have come to what we may call Egypt. They had Jesus with them, strove to render one another happy, and so we find our joy in our simple community life; we too, live on what Providence sends."

But Providence was generous with them in fertile Oregon. Their first year's harvest yielded an abundance of potatoes and pumpkins, green vegetables, meadow barley and peas for the cows. They set out fruit trees, planted chicory and coffee. The country itself was so rich in native fruits, berries, and nuts that the nuns called the adjoining forest their "pantry."

Loyola has left a description of a typical picnic which creates a nostalgic picture of simple joys on a golden day in high summer. Four of the nuns, taking their little charges with them, went to gather the low-growing wild strawberries that hid in the prairie grass, and to strip the taller bushes of their weight of berries — all the many berries in which Oregon abounded and still abounds: salmon-berries, elderberries, black-berries, huckleberries, black-caps, salal. They gathered nose-gays of flowers — flat-petaled wild rose, spears of blue iris — for their favorite saints. At noon the Sisters spread their lunch in the shade of a large pine, and just as they were seating themselves who should arrive but Baptiste "with hot pancakes sent by Sister Mary Catherine and Sister Mary Albine who were keeping house."

It was a happy day. The pupils ran here and there, away from their gentle teachers and back again with eager questions and sometimes even with offerings of their reflections, "which were rather wise for little Indian girls." And the children showed gratifying instances of their new training in manners, helping the Sisters up the hills and drawing aside the low-hanging branches that obstructed their way.

It is always pleasant to read of the six disciplined nuns indulging themselves a little. Loyola, unlike Aloysia, was apt to report these indulgences with an air of guilt. Following one of their periodic retreats we find her writing almost apologetically to Namur: "After eight days of strict silence a little feast for the Sisters was surely permissible. I made a pie with some of the dried apples from Belgium, to which I added native mulberries. The pie was delicious, and we were wishing that you could enjoy it with us."

By the end of their first year the Sisters had been able to solemnize the Month of Mary with what they did not hesitate to call "due pomp." By then their little chapel was a gracious, though rather primitive bower hung with white muslin. Through it "the wind entered in unrestrained freedom," giving a "good view of the outside," had any Sister looked up and out at the play of sun and shadow on the green world beyond their wall. The front of the altar they hung with colored paper, and the tabernacle had been draped with two old curtains brought from one of the classrooms at Namur. During the Month of Mary they made a little canopy of white muslin over the Blessed Mother and offered her lavish gifts of the wild flowers which they found far more beautiful than those of Europe.

It was while standing before this altar in their humble chapel that the six nuns presented their most touching tableau. Led off by staunch Aloysia, these gentle, loyal, hard-working Sisters compared their primitive Oregon sanctuary with the famous ones they had seen in the European world they had put from them forever.

"The altar of our Lady at Namur is not so beautiful as this," stated Aloysia unequivocally.

As she said it, all six must have thought of the miraculous statue of the Virgin in Namur — a statue so ancient that it was believed to have been brought to this holy place by none other than St. Maternus, a disciple of St. Paul. But, insisted Aloysia, none the less, even the altar at Namur could not compare.

"Nor at Ghent," chimed in Sister Norbertine.

"Nor at Ixelles," added Loyola.

So the years passed. In time their little orphans and chil-

dren of the forest could sing the Litany of our Lady and hymns
in her honor. They regularly made confession, attended Holy
Communion, opened the door for the Sisters, washed their
dusky faces daily, combed the vermin out of their own hair,
learned how to knit and sew and cook and even to read a little.
The work in Oregon progressed so well that in a few years a
reinforcement of Belgian nuns — bearing names no less tune-
ful: Renilde, Odelie, Aldegonde, Francesca — had arrived at
Oregon City to open another school.

Yet within another few years these high-souled enterprises
were to peter out. After the fateful murder of the Presbyterian
Whitmans at Waiilatpu, anti-Catholic feeling rose menacingly
in the Far West. Oregon was at last claimed by the United
States as a territory, and the prairie-schooner emigrants were
predominantly Protestant. The gold rush to California took
away many settlers. There were bad times, followed by a cholera
epidemic.

Though historic forces caught the gentle Sisters in their re-
lentless grip, they did not yield easily. When St. Paul's was
closed, they went to Oregon City and tried, by consolidation
with the reinforcements from Belgium, to weather the storm.
But times grew steadily worse. The Sisters "eked out a scanty
subsistence by sewing sacks for the mills." This could not go on
forever.

Finally, with the same combination of fortitude and insouciance with which they had departed from Belgium, the nuns
left Oregon for California. The greedy forest crept up again
on their wilderness garden and chapel. Camp smoke in time
dulled the colored pictures of Biblical scenes that the Indians
had so coveted. The venerable mission oak saw no longer Sister
Catherine "alone at the washing." The pine *"gigantesque"* was
never again to have French pancakes spread at its foot on a
summer picnic by Belgian nuns and little Indian girls with
wilted nosegays for favorite saints clutched in their dark fingers.

V. Red Women

THE WHITE WOMEN who came overland and round the Horn
to the northern shores of the Pacific in the middle of the nineteenth century, there to set up civilized communities in a virgin
country, could never have played their historic roles if it had
not been for a young Indian squaw named Sacajawea. Sacajawea helped to guide the Lewis and Clark Expedition across
America and back in 1804–6. It is now accepted as historical
fact that without this young Shoshone slave President Jefferson's two adventurous envoys, with their twenty-nine picked
men, would never have come through to the Western ocean. If
they had not won through to claim the Western territory in
the name of the United States, Great Britain's title to these rich
lands would have been much stronger. Oregon, Washington,
Idaho, Montana might never have been in the Union.

Belatedly Sacajawea has come into her own as a figure of
heroic dimension. Books have been written about her. She has
been named by James Truslow Adams, an elector of the Hall
of Fame, one of the six most important American women. Yet
to this day relatively few people know her story.

The Pacific Northwest, however, knows and honors the young
Indian mother who made possible the most important trans-
continental journey of the early nineteenth century. Sacajawea
has become the Western prototype of all pioneer females, red
as well as white, who followed her into frontier country. As far
back as the Lewis and Clark Exposition, held in Portland in
1905, Abigail Scott Duniway, the leading Western feminist,
speaking at the unveiling of Sacajawea's statue in a public
park, found in this remarkable squaw a symbol of all the un-
sung and unrewarded virtues of frontier womankind.

It was in 1804 that Meriwether Lewis and William Clark,
camping on the Missouri River, near the present city of Bis-
marck, North Dakota, making preparations for their great adventure farther to the West, had the good fortune to acquire

Sacajawea. They got her because she was the wife of the half-breed interpreter Charbonneau, whom they were taking with them on the long trip. Like most Indians and half-breeds, Charbonneau had more than one wife. It is likely that his favorite, Otter Woman, would have been taken instead of Sacajawea had her baby still been in the back-packing age. But Otter Woman's infant had grown to toddling size by the time the expedition got under way, and a toddling child on the overland trail was a manifest impossibility. Sacajawea's little son, Baptiste, newborn, could be strapped to her back for a two-year period at least.

Both of these two wives of Charbonneau were Shoshones. Both had been captured in a raid by Blackfeet and literally sold down the river, where they came eventually into the possession of Charbonneau. Legend says that the half-breed interpreter won Sacajawea for a trifle in a gambling game. Her value was to prove above price long before President Jefferson's expedition reached its final goal.

Lewis and Clark knew that they must, if possible, find and take with them a Shoshone, for when they reached the mountainous northern country they would have to have horses, not canoes, to turn westward into the unknown land watered by the legendary Oregon. The Shoshone tribe were Horse Indians, and they knew every trail and pass in the region of the Continental Divide. Although a squaw was not considered of much account among hunting tribes, Sacajawea was the best Shoshone the white men could find. They hoped to be able to use her to smooth the way with her kinsfolk.

Sacajawea's first dramatic act of cool-headedness, and the one which brought her the fervent gratitude and respect of Lewis and Clark, occurred on the upper reaches of the Missouri River. The dugout canoe in which she and her baby rode was the lead canoe. In it were stored the expedition's instruments, maps, medicine, and other vital supplies. Although Lewis and Clark must have agreed that one of them should always remain in this boat, there came a day when they were both ashore at the same time. A squall struck the pirogue, and as it keeled half-over, Charbonneau, the hysterical half-breed who was steering it, lost his head. Men shouted and cursed and tried to right the boat — made difficult by the sail it was carrying. In the turmoil Sacajawea, with the baby to save as well as herself, coolly snatched from the swirling current the precious papers and supplies.

That night in his *Journal* the grateful Clark acknowledged their debt to the little slave by recording for history that she had saved for them almost every article indispensable to the success of the enterprise, in which they were by then launched to the distance of 2,200 miles.

There were other ways, however, less dramatic, but equally important, by which Sacajawea proved helpful in the long hard pull of a two-year journey through wild new country. Explorers, facing the problem of transportation, were apt to carry into the wilderness supplies which were inadequate to keep them from dietary ills and subsequent physical collapse. They based their hopes for provisions on a land they did not know. Fortunately Sacajawea knew the hidden foods of the wilderness. She knew how to get the delicious wild artichokes from the holes where the gophers had stored them. She could dig roots of wild carrot and fennel with which to make nourishing soups. She hoarded bits of bread for her baby and brought them out to share with the men when they were ill and despondent. She knew how to break the shank bones of elk and boil them to extract tallow. When shoes gave out she could make moccasins in their stead. She even understood the pleasure of celebrations for lonely men and shared in the Christmas gift-giving on the dreary, rain-ridden Clatsop plains of Oregon by giving presents of the "white weazel tails" she had been collecting.

But perhaps her greatest contribution to the day-by-day threading of unknown waterways, pathless forests, and trackless plains was her uncanny sense of direction. Lewis and Clark had only rough Indian maps made on a stretch of deer hide to help them in traversing that tumultuous landscape which lies in the Northwest section of the continent. To Sacajawea's keen and knowing eye a countryside soon yielded the secrets by which it could be conquered. Mountains that appeared to be only row upon row of wild ridges showed her where their passes were and streams mysteriously indicated their hidden sources. Lewis and Clark learned in time to trust her implicitly, to follow without question where her pointing finger indicated.

After many days of weary travel with constant hazards they came to the "Great Divide," the place where the waters of streams and rivers no longer flowed east, but west toward the Pacific. Although she had not seen the country of her childhood for many years, with the Indian's keen memory for landmarks Sacajawea recognized the scenes of her early life the moment they entered Shoshone land. When she saw again the faces of her own people she "danced for the joyful sight," and when she found once more her long-lost brother, Cameahwait, she "ran and embraced him, throwing over him her blanket and weeping profusely."

Luckily for Lewis and Clark, Sacajawea's brother was now a chief of the tribe whose goodwill and help they must have to continue their dangerous journey. Cameahwait was impressed with the standing his sister enjoyed among these important white men. She had wept at finding him again and had made him generous gifts of such unfamiliar foods as sugar and squash. Cameahwait persuaded his people to postpone their annual buffalo hunt until they had assisted his sister's friends across the great mountain barrier and on into the Columbia Basin. Only once was there hint of treachery. Some malcontents, worried about losing their winter's food supply, wished to abandon the whites half-way through the mountains. Sacajawea discovered the plan in time, and danger was averted by Lewis, who called the leaders together and told them that the white men would not be their friends, bring them arms, or help them against their enemies if they did not keep their promise.

Sacajawea was to prove useful with tribes other than those to whom she was linked by blood bonds. Wrote Clark: "The wife of Charbonneau, our interpreter, reconciles all the Indians as to our friendly intentions. A woman with a party of men is a token of peace."

Although Sacajawea never held the title or earned the pay of an interpreter, serving in this capacity was another of her contributions to the success of the expedition. The difficulties of communication for the white men are indicated in a note in one of the journals which says: "In the first place we spoke in English to one of our men who translated it into French to Charbonneau; he interpreted it to his wife in the Minnetaree language, and she then put it into Shoshonee, and the young Shoshonee prisoner explained it to the Chopunnish in their own dialect."

Sacajawea helped break the social ice by organizing dances among the Indian tribes they encountered on the long journey to the coast. She must have been particularly interested in the dance as a means of expression, for she is credited with introducing — many years later — the Sundance to the Shoshones, a dance they subsequently made their own. Along the way Cruzatte, the expedition's fiddler, would play the most beguiling tunes he knew. York, Clark's Negro servant, would dance solos — swift sharp clogs and lazy-rhythmed shuffles, which, combined with his black face, delighted the redskins, who had never seen a Negro before. Finally the Indians would be reassured. They too would dance, softly beating the earth with the flat of their moccasined feet. Then there would follow the pipe, and friendliness.

In a journey lasting almost two and a half years and covering many thousand miles of country, Sacajawea gave the white men no trouble. Yet she was not merely a passive squaw; she possessed intelligence, will, and even charm. She had a high spirit when aroused. She is supposed to have left Charbonneau for good, later on in her career, because he struck her in front of a new, and younger, wife. What her appearance was we do not know, except that she was small in stature. Brackenridge described her in his journal as a "good creature, of a mild and gentle disposition . . . greatly attached to the whites, whose manners and airs she tries to imitate." That she earned the true affection of the leaders of the expedition is plain from their journals, in which she is referred to quaintly as "Janey." They named a river for her. She slept in the main tent. They cared for her tenderly when she was sick. There is no record that she ever complained. She asked only one "indulgence." And it is by this indulgence that zealous historians and researchers were able to trace her later life.

Sacajawea was "indulged," as Lewis put it, by being allowed while in Oregon to go with the men to view the Big Water, the Pacific Ocean. Perhaps her driving desire to see a boundless expanse of salt water came from generations of inland ancestors. Whatever her awe at the first sight of an ocean, however, it was lost in her amazement at the body of a whale cast up on the white Pacific sands. The story of the Big Fish became Sacajawea's most famous anecdote of her long trip with Lewis and Clark. Many years later — by now a squaw with another name, but still a wanderer — she was entertaining Indians of the inland tribes she visited with the tale of that dead whale she had seen on the Oregon beach. When they asked her to measure its length and she pointed out the sixty or seventy feet between her hitching post and her tepee they would yell aloud in derisive chorus: "Liar! Liar! The squaw is a liar!" Though she might describe the seals she had seen as "people who lived in the water" without being doubted, the dimensions of the whale were too much even for Indian credulity.

The legend of the traveling squaw with the whale story, together with Lewis and Clark's journals, established finally the fact that Sacajawea lived well past the time at which she is supposed to have died. She lived, indeed, to be one hundred years of age, and long enough to ride up and down and across the Western country with free passes on the early stagecoaches, visiting strange tribes. As she traveled she carried with her unprompted propaganda for the whites. Since the days of big hunting were forever over, she tried to persuade Northern Indians to learn agriculture. She had, as a matter of fact, subtly interested her own tribe in food luxuries beyond wild game, roots, and berries when she brought her brother, Cameahwait, his first taste of sugar and boiled him a mess of squash from the gardens of the Mandans.

Her son, Baptiste, the papoose she carried so many thousands of miles, inevitably became a traveler also — a world traveler. Educated by Clark in St. Louis, he was later taken to Germany by Prince Paul of Württemberg, a German adventurer of the last century. Reports have come back to this country of the presence in Stuttgart of a portrait of *Prince Paul and His Indian Boy* — no doubt destroyed under Hitler, as it would not do to show a pure-blooded Aryan consorting intimately with a red-skinned savage from the New World. Another painting does survive, however, made by Prince Paul's traveling companion, the artist Mollhausen, showing the Prince, very elegant in mutton-chop whiskers and cutaway, seated at ease in the primeval forest among naked Indians, including Sacajawea's son, with his hair "roached" and a long pipe dangling before his bare legs.

Baptiste, on his return to America, was a guide and interpreter like his mother, only with the difference that he was paid for his trouble. He turns up in journals of the period consorting with famous explorers, entertaining white travelers with mint juleps at his island home on the River Platte. But Baptiste's activities could hardly compare in importance with those of Sacajawea, who under a succession of names — Chief, Grass Woman, Lost Woman — spent her life until 1884, the year of her death, acting as an unpaid agent of goodwill from one Indian tribe to another and from whites to Indians, and Indians to whites.

The less well-known facts of Sacajawea's later years add to her stature as a significant American personality. They do not compare in importance, however, to her first great and unconscious service to the United States. In a time when a sense of the value and beauty of the lands of the Pacific Northwest is fresh in the American consciousness it must be remembered that it was an Indian woman, a "squaw," who made possible our claim to this rich section of the continent.

Sacajawea, though by far the greatest, was not the only Indian woman to play a role in opening the Western lands to the whites. In the early days white adventurers found it a necessity to take an Indian woman as a wife. For one thing, the life led by these traders, trappers, and explorers was considered too hard for any white woman to endure, and, for another, a red woman could give valuable aid to her husband. Already adapted to frontier existence, she could help him in his work, accompany him on his difficult and dangerous journeys, teach him to bargain to advantage with her own race. These Indian women knew how to live off the land. They had their own domestic economy, developed from generations of privation and experiment.

Before white women came to the West in large numbers, there was no social onus attached to marrying red women. It was taken for granted that even high officials of the fur-trading companies would marry Indians. Often these women were exceptional characters, possessing both beauty and intelligence. Tales of this period have a particularly romantic quality. Factors in their wilderness outposts lived in almost royal style, with such appurtenances as — in McLoughlin's case — a kilted Scot who was used to awe Indians and to pipe distinguished guests into the state dining-room where tables waited, loaded with luxuries from England and the choicest foods of the wilderness. McLoughlin kept his Indian wife hidden in a frontier approximation to purdah, but enough people saw her to report on her charm and grace. McDonald, a factor at Fort Colville, and also a famous host, had a wife whom the missionaries especially admired. Cautious Mr. Eells went so far as to call her a jewel.

James Birnie, another high-ranking fur company official, had a wife from the Red River settlement in Canada who ruled like a queen at Astoria in Oregon. Contemporaries reported her bearing herself "with all the self-assertion of an English dame of long pedigree." She sat at the head of her husband's table and there was no one in all the Western country who was not proud to be her guest.

[100]

RED WOMEN

Once a year Mrs. Birnie abandoned white ways and resumed her Indian character. This was when she made her annual trip to Shoalwater Bay for elk meat, clams, and cranberries. In the early autumn she would set out in her great canoe, one of the wonders of the countryside, since it could carry seventy people. Dipping their paddles in unison and chanting as they went, her party would pass the Chinook villages on their way into Chinook River to the portage; thence to Nasel River and on into Shoalwater Bay. After a few weeks of Indian life, hunting, fishing, and berry-picking, Mrs. Birnie would return in the big canoe to Birnie Hall and take up her social duties as an eminent white man's wife.

If such yarners as Joe Meek and Jim Bridger are to be believed, Indian women in the fur-trading days were happy to run off and take up life with whites. No matter how hard their existence, it could never be as hard as life with their own people. They often risked being scalped or having their tongues cut out to betray war plans and tribal secrets.

In the journal kept by Lewis and Clark an entry indicates that sometimes even the more phlegmatic Indian women of the coast regions went at least half-way in establishing friendly relations:

"An old woman & Wife to a Chief of the Chunnooks came and made a Camp near ours. She brought with her 6 young Squars (*her daughters & Neices*) I believe for the purpose of Gratifying the passions of the men of our party and receiving for those indulgences Such Small presents as She (the old woman) thought proper to accept of.

"Those people appear to view Sensuality as a Necessary evel, and do not appear to abhor it as a Crime in the unmarried State. The young females are fond of the attention of our men and appear to meet the sincere approbation of their friends and connections, for thus obtaining their favors."

Since Indians possessed a notable simplicity of attitude in regard to relations between the sexes, they did not, for the most part, look with disfavor on the mating of their beauties with men of another color and race — provided they were not per-

sonally interested at the time in the female involved. Sometimes, however, chiefs found it difficult to understand the difference between white actions toward Indian women and the
conduct exacted of Indians toward white women. Not infrequently they asked embarrassing questions as to why they
couldn't buy a blonde or a red-head they favored in some emigrant train. They had seen their own tribeswomen paid for and
carried off many times without anyone taking offense. One
old chief, observing the ardor with which white men after a
long absence from civilization wooed girls of his race, inquired
innocently if there were no white women.

It is not possible to generalize about Indian morality or the
Indian attitude toward marriage vows. Reactions varied from
tribe to tribe and from circumstance to circumstance. Some old
pioneers consider that the incident with the rebel Indian,
Leschi, which led to war in the Puget Sound country, was due
to an insult received by his sister from a white man. She had
been "married," Indian fashion, to an officer at Fort Steilacoom,
who abandoned her when his company moved on. When she
came back to her father, Chief Yanatco, the old man was over-
come with grief and humiliation. He refused to walk upright
and crept about on all fours to symbolize his degradation. For
three days he would not look on anyone, but sat alone in his
shelter howling like an animal to signify: "I am debased lower
than a dog." The young men, her brothers, then swore terrible
revenge on all whites.

Sometimes Indian girls offered themselves, sometimes they
were stolen, sometimes they were bought. Prices paid for good
Indian women varied with the need and the circumstances. In
River of No Return a story is told of a remarkable bargain in
Indian beauties as late as the year 1873. An old Nez Percé chief
offered his daughter for sale and there were three bidders. The
first offered fifty cents in cash and three deer hides. The second
gave all he had, which was three dollars and a half — presumably
also in cash. The third proffered two fishhooks. The old Indian
did not hesitate a moment. The man with the fishhooks got her
— fishhooks being difficult to obtain. The nearest source of

supply was the village of Walla Walla, two hundred miles away. Twenty years later the purchaser realized bountifully on his initial outlay. When the Nez Percé reservation was opened each Indian wife and child received 80 acres of land. The white husband of the Nez Percé beauty came into the enviable position of guardian of a family with 480 valuable acres.

Occasionally white women crossing the plains, or living in some unprotected fort, were captured and held prisoner by Indians. Oregon had its Lorinda Bewley, made captive after the Whitman massacre, who finally was ransomed back into white life, where she married, raised a family, and, in the end, lived a commonplace existence. There was also the intelligent and resourceful Fanny Kelly, whom the Sioux captured while she was traveling west. Fanny wrote an account of her adventures, *Narrative of My Captivity among the Sioux Indians*. Published in Philadelphia in 1872, it is good cinema material of the old romantic variety. Fanny finally made her escape from the Sioux unharmed — though she almost met death at the hands of a jealous wife of the old chief whose wounds she had been nursing. In her encounter with the Indian woman Fanny was exceptionally lucky, for it is known that squaws of the warlike tribes were easily aroused to fits of jealousy. Their tortures and mutilations of white women who had received attention from braves often rose to peaks of frenzy. These bloody orgies were directed at the physical features which differed from their own. They put out eyes, pulled out hair, cut off lips and breasts.

There were all kinds of Indian women in the early days in the Far West. There were the shrewd traders, like Peter Skene Ogden's wife, Julia, who is said to have ruled the Flathead Council and who through her business acumen and her family ties was largely responsible for her husband's success in frontier country. There were the self-effacing wives of the fur company officials in their distinctive costumes, "English style," with the exception of braided, beaded, or embroidered leggings of "gay color and good quality." There were the town "characters" like Olympia's Julia and Seattle's Princess Angeline. There were, of course, the legendary beauties. Finally, there were the heroines like Sacajawea, Winema, the Dorion Woman, Jane Silcott, daughter of Chief Timothy.

The Dorion Woman, among heroines, ranks next to Sacajawea. Her husband also was an interpreter who came west with the Hunt Expedition, bound for Astoria. Almost all the members of this ill-fated party perished en route. When hostile Indians set upon the remnants of the group with whom she was traveling, the Dorion Woman managed to escape with her two small children. She fled into the Blue Mountains of eastern Oregon without weapons, food, or tools, and there she built a shelter, killed for meat the horse on which she had escaped, and managed to live through the winter's snows. In the spring she dragged herself across the mountains to a friendly Indian camp, both her children still miraculously alive.

Jane, the daughter of Timothy, the converted chief in whom Spalding, the missionary, found a friend, is honored in the Inland Empire. Jane was sent by her father to guide a party of whites into the gold country at Orofino, thus starting the stampede into that part of the West. Why this was such an act of noble service as to make Jane worthy of a place alongside the Dorion Woman and Sacajawea is not quite clear, but there she is often placed. There is also a story that Jane's father had ferried the troops of Colonel Steptoe across the Snake when they were fighting Indians in the Palouse country, and Jane, among other Indian women, helped tend the white wounded. This was purest treachery to their own race and not so easy to admire when viewed in historical perspective.

Oregon honors a woman named Winema, who at the time of the Indian uprisings in the southern part of the state saved the life of a Reservation Superintendent at the risk of her own. This heroine of the picturesque and bloody Modoc War, which was waged in the weird frozen turbulence of the lava beds, married a white man and learned the language so well that she became an interpreter. Winema is unique among Indian heroines in that she was rewarded during her lifetime for her loyalty and devotion. Congress actually voted her a pension, and the

RED WOMEN

D.A.R. erected over her grave a tablet reading: "Winema --
The Strong Heart."

As to Indian "beauties," whether they were beautiful by
modern standards is open to some doubt. They must often have
looked beautiful to men who had not seen a woman of any color
or stripe for many months. At Spokane House, a famous trading
post of the early nineteenth century, there was a ballroom in
one of the buildings where Indian belles and white men could
dance together. Alexander Ross, a Scotch trader, wrote that
there were "no females in the land so fair to look upon as the
nymphs of Spokane; no damsels could dance so gracefully as
they; none were so attractive." In the Boise, Idaho, *News* of
1863 there appeared a description of the daughter of the Nez
Percé chief, Lawyer, written in language that verged on the
rapturous. The bride was reported moving toward the altar
"clothed in blushes of modesty and superbly worked leggings
all covered with precious gems and other kinds of beads. . . .
She wore no hoops but allowed her own development of form
to fill the outlines where others less perfect have to depend on
hoops and cottons."

It was perhaps because of literary ecstasies similar to these
that Horace Wirtz, a witty surgeon residing at Fort Steilacoom
in 1858, wrote his *Lines to a Klootchman,* couching in the elaborate form of an ode his ironical recognition of the white man's
attraction to the Indian woman. These highly prized verses
appear as rare items in the scrapbooks of the oldest pioneers.
They are worth reproducing as a period piece.

LINES TO A KLOOTCHMAN

by Sitkum Siwash, Esq.

Sweet nymph! although of dirtier hue thou art
Than other ladies brought from eastern clime
To thee I yield the tribute of my love,
To thee I dedicate these humble rhymes.
And if too faint I string my trembling lyre
Sweet Pocahontas! thou my verse inspire.

WESTWARD THE WOMEN

Long time whilom I thought that pallid cheeks
And blue eyes smiling like the sky at morn,
And auburn curls and fingers rosy-tipped,
Comprised all beauty that of earth was born;
But other charms, exceeding all of these
I've found at last on far Pacific seas.

Where Puget Sound its placid waters spreads
And Steilacoom uplifts its bosky shore
Paddling the light canoe, the maid I met
Whose modest graces did enchant me more
Than all the pictures fair by poets wrought
In golden dreams and raptured moods of thought.

Thy well-squeezed head was flat as flounders are,
Thy hair with dog-fish oil resplendent shone
Thy feet were bare and slightly inward turned,
And e'en I ween of stockings thou hads't none;
But beauty's presence beamed from every part,
Though unadorned by trickery and art.

A blanket red, that had seen better days
Around thy shoulders gracefully was twined;
And eke a petticoat that once was clean,
Thy slender waist and swelling limbs did bind;
A mild but fishy odor round thee clung
As though dried salmon thou hads't been among.

And thus it was; for in the savage home
Where Indian wigwams look o'er waters blue
The custom is to spear the speckled fish
And smoke them when there's nothing else to do;
For huckleberries are a watery food,
And clams and oysters are not always good.

But though thou smellest strong of salmon dry
Though innocent of soap thy hands appear;
Although thy toes turn inward with a curl
And though thy skull is smashed from front to rear;
Though nameless animals thy hair infest
Still do I love thee of all maidens best.

Then give me but a blanket and a mat
Dried clams and fish my only food shall be

RED WOMEN

My only house a half-upturned canoe,
Whiskey my drink, and love alone for thee;
Then fair-haired dames for me will vainly shine,
In all the charms of hoops and crinoline.

In all justice to the Idaho gentleman's descriptive flight, as opposed to Mr. Wirtz's satire, it must be said that the inland Indian woman was an object of far greater charm than the squaw from the coast. Coast red women had flattened heads and bodies deformed by exercise in canoes. The fish oil they used so freely on the person added nothing to their magnetism. Perhaps the Idaho gentleman who was so affected by the charms of the Nez Percé Princess, had a grievance against some nameless white female, for in the same newspaper he aired his opinion of white women in a description which could hardly have been applicable to anyone in a pioneer community. Taking a deep breath, he intoned: "Ye pining, screwed-up, wasp-waisted, putty-faced, consumption-mortgaged and novel-devouring daughters of fashion and idleness, you are no more fit for matrimony than a pullet is to look after a family of fifteen chickens."

Every Western town had a favorite Indian character, and some of them were women. In late pioneer days Olympia, Washington, had its Julia, who is remembered for following the newly-come and still novel Salvation Army through the maple-shaded streets of the sedate state capital. Full of high spirits — both natural and alcoholic — she accompanied the drumbeats with piercing yells, embarrassing the citizenry and the Army equally by appealing to all men seen en route: "Come along, all you fellahs, come along to Jesus!"

Seattle had the Princess Angeline, daughter of the good chief Seattle, always a friend to the whites. In her old age Angeline, dirty, ancient, withered like a dried fruit, with her baskets for sale beside her, spent hours seated on the curbstone in Pioneer Square in the city named for her father. "She's a princess," people liked to whisper, pointing her out to strangers, enjoying to the full that sense of life's dramatic flux — so low are the mighty fallen!

Angeline had a daughter, Betsy, who came to a more tragic end than her mother, and many years before. A white man, said to be "the son of a minister and well brought up," bought her. She had a child by him, "a fine little boy" — so wrote an early minister's wife, recounting the tale to distant Eastern relatives. Betsy, however, never cared for her husband or the white way of life. Rumor said that the man, in spite of his genteel antecedents, sometimes beat her. After the baby came he was reputedly kinder, but one day when he was at work Betsy hanged herself in their cabin. The unfortunate man buried her whitestyle, following the body on foot to the grave, supported by the company of two other local squaw-men. As soon as she was in the earth, the Indians took over and set up their ritualistic howling and wailing. The husband fled the community, well aware that, as he had been responsible for the disgrace of a suicide, the Indians would seek an opportunity to kill him. He also knew that he had stepped permanently outside the pale of white society when he chose to mate with an Indian in the face of community disapproval. He had effectively shut the doors to both worlds.

Since white females, for the most part, looked down on squaws, it was not until the post-pioneer period that Indian women began to assume their rightful place in Western history. Then much of the interest they aroused stemmed from the wave of feminism following in the wake of the first female pioneers. Red women too, as well as white, were suddenly perceived to have been responsible for man's conquest of the wilderness. Unpaid for their services, like Sacajawea, personally unrecognized in spite of their courage and practical wisdom, as were also many pioneer mothers, they began to make an appeal to such sincere Western feminists as Eva Emery Dye and Abigail Scott Duniway.

Through her novel on the Lewis and Clark Expedition, *The Conquest*, Mrs. Dye is credited with resurrecting the legend of Sacajawea and in starting the research which proved this legend to be historical fact. At the Centennial Exposition commemorating the great adventures of Lewis and Clark, held in Port-

land in 1905, a day was set aside to honor the Far Western suf-
fragist Mrs. Duniway. Her work on behalf of the rights of
women was considered as worthy of recognition as the achieve-
ments of those practical visionaries in another field, Meriwether
Lewis and William Clark. Mrs. Duniway responded to the
honor by writing a Centennial Ode, in which, on behalf of
Oregon women, she paid tribute to Sacajawea:

> And then, to make the prophecy complete,
> An Indian mother led the devious way,
> Foreshadowing woman's place, which man shall greet
> Without a protest, in a hastening day,
> When womanhood, benignant, wise and free,
> Shall lead him to yet greater heights of strength and victory.

It has long been an American pose to be bored with the Indian, an attitude which probably has its roots in over-exposure
to *Hiawatha* in grade school, or to the eagle-plumed yaa-yaa
"chiefs" and "princesses" who beat drums and floor boards on
vaudeville circuits early in the century. Somehow the noble red
man always emerged a comic or a pokerface whenever presented
in fiction or drama. It is good to find — from contemporary accounts — that blood flowed warmly in the veins of Northwest
squaws at least: Julia drank too much from an excess of high
spirits, Betsy killed herself because she did not care for her
husband, Sacajawea struck an importunate white suitor with
a shank of elk, Mrs. Birnie snubbed her social inferiors, Mrs.
McDonald's table manners were perfect by Maine standards,
Peter Skene Ogden's Julia drove a hard bargain, Yanatco's
daughter went home to her father, Jane Silcott upbraided her
husband for letting her carry in wood while he played cards.
. . . These women were all women and the color of their skin
was incidental.

VI. Females Are Sought

In 1846 when Narcissa Whitman sat in her wilderness house at Waiilatpu and wrote to her sister in far-away up-state New York, she urged her to make the long journey westward to the new country that lay beyond the Great American Desert and the Rocky Mountains. She wrote: "Bring as many girls as you can, but let every young man bring a wife, for he will want one after he gets here, if he never did before."

Narcissa was apparently unaware of the irony of her remarks. Only a few years before in penning her own humble request to the mission board to be allowed to travel west to Christianize the Indians, she had questioned doubtfully: Are females wanted?

By the 1860's another cultivated resident of the Pacific Northwest made significant note of the novel attitude of men toward women on the lonely frontier. In a brief but charming book with a very long title, *Life at Puget Sound with Sketches of Travel in Washington Territory, British Columbia, Oregon and California,* Caroline Leighton, a gentle New England lady declared:

> "Among the miners of the upper country, who had not seen a white woman for a year, I received such honors that I am afraid I should have had a very mistaken impression of my importance if I had lived among them. At every stopping-place they made little fires in their frying-pans, and set them around me, to keep off the mosquitoes, while I took my meal. As the columns of smoke rose about me, I felt like a heathen goddess, to whom incense was being offered."

Caroline Leighton, sitting among the smoky offerings of the Idaho miners, was symbolic. Men in the Far West were lonely. They wanted women. They needed women. Some men reacted simply and instinctively to the need. Others, more developed, saw an importance in the presence of women that went deeper than the personal. Among these was the Reverend Mr. H. K. W. Perkins, who wrote a shrewd analysis of the character of

Narcissa Whitman in a letter to her sister. He found Narcissa adapted by nature to a wholly "different destiny. She longed for society, refined society. She was intellectually & by association fitted to do good only in such a sphere. . . . The self-denial that took her away from it was suicidal." After several paragraphs in the same style the Reverend Mr. Perkins, who admitted quite frankly that he could live happily in a wigwam all his life and found the Indian manner of living both sensible and appealing, penned a sentence which summed up the role that women of gentle breeding unconsciously played in frontier America:

"Certain it is that we needed such minds to keep us in love with civilized life, to remind us occasionally of home."

Elkanah Walker, in a letter he wrote to his absent wife, left a fair picture of the combination servant and companion that the average man in new country dreamt of having for himself:

"I am tired of keeping an old bachelor's hall. Things do not go to suit me when I come in from work tired almost to death. I want someone to get me a good supper & let me take my ease & when I am very tired in the morning I want someone to get up & get breakfast & let me lay in bed & take my rest. More than all I want my wife where I can have her company & to cheer me up when the blue devils chain me down. . . ."

The presence of white women in increasing numbers after the first missionary wives dared the rigors of seven months' travel by horseback made the marriages of Indian squaws and white men socially unacceptable. Further than this, the Donation Land Act of 1850, which gave a man and his wife 640 acres of homestead, "a mile square of land," succeeded in booming the female market sky-high. Far Western girls were hardly out of their teens before they were snatched up by importunate young men who wanted not only land but heirs, pies like mother used to make, and companions in their solitude. The bachelors' "unseemly race" through the counties of Oregon, indiscriminately proposing matrimony to "tearful widows of a fortnight and to little girls busy with mud pies," was held up to ridicule by Abigail Duniway and others, but nothing stopped them. They seemed to have lost all judgment and whatever sense of fitting conduct they might have once possessed.

Many eager men thought nothing of riding their Cayuse ponies right up to the doors of respectable Portland houses, remaining in the saddle and rapping on the door with a stick (there were no sidewalks in their way in those days). They would sit jingling their Mexican spurs until the housewife appeared. "Good morning to you, ma'am, are you married?" they would ask. If the reply was yes they tipped their hats and went on. If it was no they immediately proposed. A woman who described the scene said that she retorted to one such visitor — after answering that she was not married but did not care to consider his offer — that she did not know what use she had for him unless she should put him behind the stove and break bark over his head.

It was perhaps this land-claim frenzy that left it a mild disgrace in the Far West to be a bachelor. It is not easy to trace the origin of this stigma, but that it was so old-timers have left indisputable record. A typical story about the dreaded condition of bachelorhood is that of a young man who sold his entire claim for a gold watch, after the girl he left behind was wooed and won on her way to the West by another suitor "with lots of cows." Not only did the rejected suitor refuse to live alone and be called a bachelor, but in turn the man to whom he sold the land also would not "batch" and be called a bachelor, so he never lived on the tract he bought.

Old-timers recall that it was considered a sort of disgrace to be a bachelor, "kind of lower caste" — though they don't see why, as there were very few ladies around and plenty of single men. That gentle Christian, Eliza Spalding, began a paragraph in her journal: "Let me say a good word for the bachelors," thus implying that good words were scarce for these unnatural creatures.

The term "old batch" carries to this day a definite, though not necessarily harsh opprobrium in Western vernacular. It creates at once the picture of an unkempt grizzle-beard with mild vagaries. The Western country, because of its space and solitude, has always invited and harbored that curious human creature the hermit. Hermits are still to be found up lonely canyons, gulches, or rivers, on mountain tops, in ghost towns.

The Oregon cattleman Bill Hanley wrote a description of an old miner he saw as he rode after nightfall through one of the deserted mining towns that dot the Western country. Hearing an eerie sound of music and seeing a gleam of light, he got off his horse to investigate. He pushed open the door of a ramshackle building and found a little wizened man all alone in a big, rough, neglected room, lit dingily by a piece of braided calico in a tin plate of tallow, playing a tune on a flute.

"There sat the little old fellow dreaming out loud with his flute. . . . Old fellow around sixty or seventy with the little flute that had been his companion forever, laying around on gravel beds. . . . Now in this old camp, the last one, just to stay until someone found him and hauled him off to the poorhouse. . . . His life wasn't dingy, no matter what your interpretation of it might be. The ordinary traveler coming along would say what an awful life this fellow has . . . but it wasn't awful at all, for he was living in his dream and making music to it . . . With the old miner . . . hope grows stronger as life grows weaker. His life is a very happy one for his myths are like opiates."

The men, however, who had no myths for opiates and found flutes poor company determined to do something about living alone. Since these were the days before matrimonial bureaus, Asa Mercer, a young man of Washington Territory, decided to set about personally solving the problem which so obviously existed in frontier country where girls were so scarce that when dances were given in some communities every man who brought a girl got in free, and anyone turning up with extra females received twenty-five cents a head for his benefaction. Essays had been appearing from the first in Northwest newspapers on such subjects as "Scarcity of White Women," "Need of Good Wives." Finally in 1860 the *Puget Sound Herald* of Steilacoom advertised an open meeting to which all bachelors were invited in order to discuss their dilemma. Out of this first meeting came further meetings and at last Asa's bold plan to import eligible women from the Eastern states by way of a journey round the Horn.

"Attention, Bachelors: Believing that our only chance for a realization of the benefits and early attainments of matrimonial alliances depends upon the arrival in our midst of a number of the fair sex from the Atlantic states, and that, to bring about such an arrival a united effort and action are called for on our part, we respectfully request a full attendance of all eligible and sincerely desirous bachelors of this community to assemble on Tuesday evening next, February 28th, in Delin and Shorey's building to devise ways and means to secure this much-needed and desirable emigration to our shore."

Although there is no record that Asa Mercer knew it, there was actually an American precedent for his bold plan. In the seventeenth century several cargoes of girls from England, "agreeable persons, young and incorrupt," came to the Virginia colony and were eagerly bought up at the boat landing by lonely planters who paid one hundred and twenty pounds of tobacco — worth roughly eighty dollars — for a bride. In most respects the Far West traces its traditions of conduct to New England, but in this instance it breaks sharply with Puritan precedent, for the New England colonists headed their catalogue of desperately needed items from the old country — such as copper kettles, tame turkeys, peas, and beans — with "ministers." Virginia frankly headed its list: "wives."

So essential was Asa's plan considered in the Far West that funds would have been made available from the public treasury for his journey had the treasury not been empty. He had, however, the full backing of William Pickering, the Governor of Washington Territory, his own brother, Judge Thomas Mercer, and many another influential citizen.

Asa laid his plans carefully. He would not go into New England communities and crudely talk about matrimonial chances in the Pacific Northwest. He would present to the young women of New England a picture of the opportunities this developing country extended to schoolteachers, nurses, music-teachers, dressmakers, and housekeepers.

He was able on his first trip to sell his idea to eleven young women of New England, who came seven thousand miles round the Horn in the spring of 1864 and were, for the most part, snapped up at once as brides. On the strength of this modest coup Asa Mercer was elected unanimously to the upper house of the Territorial Legislative Assembly.

Fired by this initial success, Asa decided to try again on a larger scale. Very soon he was signing contracts which read:

"I, Asa Mercer, of Seattle, Washington Territory, hereby agree to bring a suitable wife, of good moral character and reputation from the East to Seattle on or before September 1865, for each of the parties whose signatures are hereunto attached, they first paying to me or my agent the sum of three hundred dollars, with which to pay the passage of said ladies from the East and to compensate me for my trouble."

Asa was not interested in making a fortune on his venture, but he did want the event to become one of national significance. He decided to offer homes and employment to the wives and orphans of Civil War soldiers.

As a boy of five, back home in Illinois, he had been dandled on the knee of Abraham Lincoln and he felt sure that he would be granted an audience with the President. But unfortunately his arrival in the East coincided almost exactly with the assassination of Lincoln. Thus Asa had to turn elsewhere for help. He got it from the Governor of Massachusetts, John A. Andrews, "the most talked about and seemingly the most popular and influential man and politician in the country." Andrews thought Mercer's idea a sound one. He introduced the brisk young man from the Far West to Edward Everett Hale.

Asa was then passed along from one important man to another in the big cities, receiving verbal encouragement in some quarters, sharp attack in others, and very little substantial help. In Washington, after weeks of the inevitable run-around, he finally got the ear of Ulysses S. Grant, who had served as a soldier in the unsettled stretches of the Far West and knew what Mercer was talking about. Grant was able, on his personal voucher, to get Mercer an order for a steamship to carry five hundred women from New York to Seattle. This order, however, the Quartermaster General refused to accept. He found it illegal, sharing perhaps the timidity of President Johnson and his Cabinet, who approved Asa's scheme but feared the moral responsibility involved. Eventually, under pressure, the Quartermaster General yielded enough to offer Mercer a 1,600-ton ship for eighty thousand dollars spot cash.

This was a sum far beyond the reach of Mercer's purse, but he found a man who had it in his hand and was ready to spend it on what seemed to him a good commercial venture — not because of the cargo of women, but because of the value of a ship on the West coast. This man was Ben Holladay, the fabulous entrepreneur and high-liver of Portland, Oregon. Holladay offered to buy the boat and let Mercer ship his cargo of females at the nominal price.

Believing that his troubles were over, Mercer went about happily giving his scheme wider publicity. He inserted a card in the *New York Times* that set out to explain the conditions in the Pacific Northwest which made such a venture feasible. Using the past tense, he wrote: "Churches and schools there were, but the great elevating, refining and moralizing element, — true woman, — was wonderfully wanting. Not that the ladies of Washington Territory were less pure and high-minded than those of any other land, but the limited number of them left the good work greater than they could perform."

Asa, in bustling about New England, was not always received with open arms. What Connecticut and New Hampshire had to say is not recorded, but the *New York Times* reported that Massachusetts newspapers ridiculed the women who considered embarking on the venture and warned them not to allow themselves to "be lost among the Amarugens," as they called the inhabitants of Washington Territory. On the whole, the *New York Times* was kind to Mercer's scheme, headlining it warmly: "Brilliant Prospect for the Settlers and Miners of the Pacific Slope." But the *New York Herald* took another stand. Warning that the whole scheme was obviously intended to fill Western houses of ill-fame with the flower of New England womanhood, it managed to bring about a number of cancellations. In the end the boat set sail under the most chaotic conditions with one hundred passengers instead of the five hundred expected.

One of the women from Lowell, Massachusetts, who made the trip with her mother and became a resident of Whidby Island, in Washington, was able to recall the details of it many years later in an article for the *Washington Historical Quarterly*. Flora Engle found on boarding Holladay's bargain vessel that "nothing had been done to the steamer since it was last used for transporting soldiers, except, possibly a partial fumigation." Mr. Mercer, not so dashing as he was when he left the West coast, hid out in a coal bin until they were well out to sea.

The food on the trip, according to Mrs. Engle, was disgraceful — everywhere, that is, but at the captain's table. Mercer, upon his emergence from the hold, took his meals with the captain until the hungry and disgruntled passengers convinced him that his conduct was tactless to say the least. After that Asa shared with his charges the fried salt beef, the tea steeped in sea water, and — at one seventeen-day stretch — the slightly parboiled beans, the main dinner dish. At one point in the journey a distracted New England housewife obtained permission to go into the galley and bake some Massachusetts gingerbread. There was a can of strawberry preserves on board that was still tenderly remembered by one passenger at least fifty years later. Whenever the passengers threatened to make trouble over their fare, some timid soul, raised on New England sea stories, would always stop them with the whispered argument: "Hush, you might incite mutiny."

So they endured. And perhaps their limited rations were a blessing in disguise, said the lady who wrote down the chronicle for posterity. There was no seasickness among them, after the first day or two, on the whole 7,000-mile trip, and this might have been due to the fact that their stomachs had nothing to disgorge.

In spite of the rations, life on shipboard was pleasant and even exciting. There was constant diversion. A young reporter, Rod, of the *New York Times,* who had gone along to write up the expedition, diverted himself by paying court to one after another of the eligible young girls. In the end every one of them rejected him. What was the matter with Rod? The chronicler fails to state. Certainly Rod's dispatches to the *Times* are disappointing. He had little to say about his companions after a first description of their conduct during a squall. He was particularly unfeeling about the terrified young woman who begged the captain on her knees to put her ashore in a rowboat. Rod hints nothing of personal adventures aboard ship and saves all his impassioned phrasing for a description of the harbor of Rio de Janeiro. Were it not for Flora Engle we should never guess, in turning the thin, stained pages of the *New York Times* of eighty years ago, that this young man with a Baedeker mind had been both ardent and unlucky with Mercer's girls.

But though Rod was unlucky, the "sly young archer, Cupid," was not idle. Mercer himself fell under the spell of a Baltimore belle named Annie Stephens. Happily "his passion was reciprocated." There were four other bona fide romances resulting in marriage at the journey's end. Some young women, fearing that they might be accused of setting out on a deliberate matrimonial venture, were extremely careful to give no encouragement to the men on shipboard. One in particular awed the company at the outset by announcing that she intended to "clothe herself in her reserve, throw herself back upon her dignity, and remain so." They had reason to believe later, commented Mrs. Engle, that her prop had given way.

One young lady with more fire than prudence got into trouble with the captain. When he gave orders for all officers to remain in their quarters "since he was disgusted with the daily doings of his engineers," the young miss made a chalk line on the deck near the saloon door and wrote above it: "Officers not allowed aft." For this piece of cheek she was confined to her room by the captain — locked in.

In California the party lost some of its members. "What inducements," says the loyal Mrs. Engle, "some of them found to remain in California I do not pretend to say."

That there were many inducements offered them to remain is clear from such a bit of evidence as a poem published in a

FEMALES ARE SOUGHT

San Francisco paper. Paraphrasing Tennyson's *Charge of the Light Brigade,* and exaggerating the number of females rather remarkably, the unknown poet of the Golden Gate published the following:

Husbands to the right of them
Husbands to the left of them
Husbands behind them
Now badgered and thundered.
Stormed at with words so fell
What shall their feelings tell?
There goes the steamer's bell,
Back from the Golden Gate
All that was left of them,
Went the 700.

Oh when can their glory fade
Oh the wild charge they made,
All the town wondered.
Honor the charge they made,
Honor the bright brigade
Sweet 700.

The majority of the party came up the coast to the Northwest in a new clean ship with good engines and a good cook. At Cape Flattery they met their first welcoming committee, a band of Indians in canoes, coming to gape, to sell fish, and incidentally to startle some of the more delicate ladies by the unconcerned scantiness of their attire.

It didn't take Mercer's girls long to settle into their new life. They taught school, they married, they raised children, they "grew up with the country." They had served to advertise the Pacific Northwest in a way no other enterprise could have done, and Asa Mercer — for all the personal attacks he had had to endure — must have been well satisfied with this part of his ambitious program.

Although Mercer's girls did not adequately fill the need for women in the Pacific Northwest, they undoubtedly helped, by the publicity they received, toward an eventual solving of the man-woman ratio in the coast section of Oregon and Washington. Inland country had its special problems. *Idaho Lore* relates that well toward the end of the century women, because of their scarcity, were still getting so much attention that many a shooting occurred over a careless exchange of glances. This situation led an Idaho editor to announce in the columns of his paper that he wanted it known that from that day henceforth he was not going to acknowledge so much as a speaking acquaintance with any man's wife and would accept no further introductions to married women.

But to balance the picture of miners burning smudges to ward off mosquitoes, men standing, hat in hand, reverently in awe at sight of a white female, there are little stories in another vein. White women were still scarce when the following incident occurred, and certainly no comment need be added to this account of unchivalrous conduct on the part of men in Washington's territorial days:

> "Mother started for Olympia on the little sidewheeler Lily; but when she was almost there — in fact in The Narrows — the little boat sank. She never forgave the men on the boat; for they all scrambled into a small boat and rowed away, leaving mother and a few others up to their armpits in water for nearly 24 hours!"

In one of the books of that remarkable woman Frances Fuller Victor, who contributed so much research, knowledge, and writing ability to the Bancroft histories, there is a scornful denial of the theory that women were "idealized and idolized" in the early days. Mrs. Victor puts into the mouth of the heroine of her story *The New Penelope* these words: "On this coast, in early times, and more or less even now, men found they could dispense with homes; they had been converted into nomads, to whom earth and sky, a blanket and a frying pan were sufficient for their needs. Unless we came to them armed with endurance to battle with primeval nature we became burdensome."

By 1872 the *Idaho World* could publish an extravagant satire indicating that, with women less scarce, admiration and reverence were distinctly on the decline:

"Take ninety pounds of flesh and bone, mainly bone, wash clean and bore holes in the ears, bend the neck to conform with the Grecian bend, the Boston dip, the kangaroo droop, the Saratoga slope or the bullfrog beak, as the taste inclines. Then add three yards of linen, one hundred yards of ruffles and seventy-five yards of edging, eighteen yards of dimity, one pair silk or cotton hose with patent hip attachment, one pair of false calves, six yards of flannel, embroidered, one pair Balmoral boots with heels three inches high, four pounds whalebone in strips, seventeen hundred and sixty yards of steel wire, three-quarters of a mile of tape, ten pounds of raw cotton or two wire hemispheres, one wire basket that would hold a bushel, four copies of the *World*, one hundred and fifty yards of silk or other dress goods, five hundred yards of lace, fourteen hundred yards fringe and other trimmings, twelve gross of buttons, one box pearl face powder, one saucer of carmine and an old hare's foot, one bush of false hair frizzed and fretted *a la maniaque*, one bundle Japanese switches with rats, mice, and other varmints, one peck of hairpins, one lace handkerchief, nine inches square with patent holder. Perfume with attar of roses or 'Blessed Baby,' or 'West End.' Stuff the head with fashionable novels, ball tickets, playbills, wedding cards, some scandal, a lot of wasted time and very little sage. Add a half grain of common sense, three scruples of religion and a modicum of modesty. Season with vanity, affectation and folly. Garnish with earrings, fingerrings, breastpins, chains, bracelets, feathers and flowers to suit the taste. Pearls and diamonds may be added and pinchbeck from the dollar store will do.

"Whirl all around in a fashionable circle and stew by gaslight for six hours.

"This dish is highly ornamental, a *piece de resistance* for the head of your table upon grand occasion, but being somewhat indigestible and highly expensive is not commended for daily consumption in the home."

This was the sort of libel of Western womanhood that caused full-blown feminists to snort with rage. Where was such a fabulous creature to be found as thus described, Abigail Scott Duniway and Bethenia Owens-Adair would ask heatedly. The wives they knew were all without exception "servants without wages and all-around drudges." By the 1870's there was beginning to blow up in the Pacific Northwest a strong wind of Equal Rights for Women.

VII. $1 a Dance

IN THE YEAR 1812 a yellow-haired, blue-eyed, and pink-cheeked girl named Jane Barnes, tending bar in Portsmouth, England, caught the fancy of one of the men who came to drink the ale and porter she served with such dash and allure in the gloomy public house of the old seacoast town. It was nothing unusual for Jane's youthful freshness to attract the attention of patrons, but in this case it led her straight to the pages of history, in which, it seems likely, even self-assured Jane could hardly have imagined herself playing any role at all, large or small.

The gentleman whose eyes fell possessively upon the vivacious barmaid was one Donald McTavish, about to set sail on a thirteen months' journey to America. He was bound for the Indian country of the Pacific Northwest, there to act as Governor of a post for the North West Company, which was hoping to push out the upstart Americans trying for a foothold to secure furs and other booty at Astoria on the Columbia River. Donald McTavish was able — though history does not tell us how — to persuade Jane that there was little future in the life of a barmaid and that anything was better than growing old prosaically in sleepy Portsmouth. He sent her out on the town to buy herself whatever she fancied in costumes for the journey. She did so well that a year and a month later her ravishing appearance led an Indian Prince — the son of a Northwest chief — to offer as high as a hundred otter skins to her relatives, and any amount of fat salmon, anchovies, elk, and pipe tobacco for her own consumption, if she would consent to be his wife.

Not only was Jane Barnes the first white woman to set foot in the Pacific Northwest; she was also the first of a class of women — the adventuresses — who were to follow and not infrequently put Western frontier communities at loggerheads and swords' points by their very physical presence. Jane was a fitting precursor to this long list of females who came to the Northwest for the ride and for possible profits to be made off women-hungry men who knew what they wanted and were willing to pay high for it. She passed from the protection of McTavish to that of Alexander Henry, a gentleman already in residence at Fort George, and when both gentlemen were drowned in an unfortunate accident, she put in her time, until the day when she set sail with a gallant skipper for Canton, tantalizing Indians as well as whites with her European trousseau worn on the wild Oregon beach where she took her solitary walks. Her further adventures in the fabulous country of Cathay have not been recorded. The last heard of Jane was in a bill presented to a London legal firm on behalf of a gentleman who wanted to collect for paying her way home from China. The correspondence regarding this matter also asked where the "poor woman" should apply for the annuity promised her, presumably, by her first protector. Whether Jane collected or not we do not know.

More than half a century was to pass before women of Jane's intrepid, carefree, and single-purposed character appeared in the Pacific Northwest in large numbers. When they came, they came overland, following the trail of prospectors for gold. Because the Pacific Northwest is associated in the American mind with the early pioneer farmers of Oregon, it is easy to overlook how much a part of this section is taken up with desert and mountain country and the rough romantic history of mining booms. Montana, Wyoming, California, and Nevada have produced frontier heroines who have properly made their way into fiction and the cinema. The equally doughty heroines of the gold saga of Idaho and the eastern sections of Washington and Oregon have been singularly neglected. Yet a roster of their names alone is inviting. The names range from the imperious dignity of such titles as the Irish Queen and the Cornish Queen, to the piquancy of Spanish Rose, Molly b' Damn, and the Little Gold Dollar, and finally to the more graphic appellations of Em' Straight-Edge, Peg-Leg Annie, Velvet Ass Rose, and Contrary Mary. (As to the last, her name, it seems, was entirely unwarranted. From all accounts she was a thoroughly affable girl.)

There was a particular raciness and picturesqueness reflected in the names miners gave the girls in parlor houses and hurdy-gurdy halls. A certain pictorial turn of phrase, peculiar to mining country, seems to be passing slowly from the language, though Idaho is still rich in the unique quality of its speech. Idahoans "fork" a horse when they mount it, they are often "busier 'n Hattie's flea," "clear grit" is to them the genuine article, and they sometimes find their fellow citizens "big as a skinned mule and twice as homely." Every old town has its collection of tantalizing local personages. The wandering questioner still hears unlikely tales of Jack the Dude, Johnny Behind the Rock, Diamond-Field Jack Davis, Coal Oil Georgie, Three-Fingered Bill Hill, Senator Few Clothes, and Jimmy the Harp — friends of the parlor house girls.

The point about both heroes and heroines of the frontier years of the Pacific Northwest is that there are plenty of people still alive to tell what they remember about them. Their day was, really, only yesterday. Settle down opposite some willing old-timer who leans far back in his chair, with the legs at an alarming angle, and he will proceed to tell, without censor and with the absolute unselfconsciousness of the true frontiersman, anything he can recall of life as he lived it. He sees no reason to present his memories in a false light or to minimize the robust charms of the period which boasted many "sporting women," pimps, "professors," gamblers, and gunmen, who were sometimes celebrities and always characters.

But first off, about the women, he wants to get something straight. They were "good" women — make no mistake about that! They were as good women as you could find anywhere and lots of 'em married well and made the best wives in the country. As to what he means by "good," it turns out to have its base in certain Christian virtues that have fallen into sad disuse. Probably the most universally admired virtue of these "fallen women" was their Good Samaritanism. They did unto others as they would others would do unto them. So what did the morals of the Irish Queen matter in a frontier country where people hadn't yet had the necessary leisure to set up social codes, as compared to the fact that she would "wade through snow up to her crotch in mid-winter to take soup to some poor devil to whom she didn't owe a damn thing. Just a heart of gold and nothing else!"

A heart of gold was what Molly b' Damn of the Coeur d'Alenes also had. Her way of showing it was a trifle eccentric at times — but people in her own milieu understood her well enough. If a miner came to town from the hills with his entire diggings for a season in his pockets — amounting to around a thousand dollars — and left Molly's in the morning without a cent, no one grew exercised on his behalf. The victim himself accepted the cleaning philosophically. "Men paid cash for provisions in those days." But when this same prospector returned to the hills and fell sick with mountain fever — which was really tick fever, we now know — and Molly b' Damn gave up business and went to nurse him back to health, then she proved herself a good woman, and people remembered her for it.

Peg-Leg Annie was another whose deed of heroism has won her a niche in Idaho's printed lore. Peg-Leg Annie didn't walk into a mining camp; she rode in, aged four, on her father's back. By the time she was a grown girl she was no better in some ways than she needed to be. One autumn with a friend and companion, Dutch Emma, she set out to cross Bald Mountain from Rocky Bar to Atlanta. An early and bitter snowstorm came up, in which the two women lost their way. Dutch Emma gave out, and though Annie had the strength to save herself, she stayed beside her dying companion, even taking off her own warm underclothes to protect her friend. Annie was found later by a searching party, snow-blind, half-crazed, and badly frozen, beside the body of her friend. They carried her back to the town of Atlanta and proceeded to amputate her legs. Idaho old-timers will have no truck with the facts of the case, which seem to be that a doctor got there in time to do the job. They will tell you, one and all, that a local amateur hacked them off with a meat saw and Annie had nothing to sustain her but a generous shot of whisky.

It's only people who do research for W.P.A. guide books who bother with such unimportant details as whether the doctor got there or didn't. Annie was a heroine, wasn't she? Without a doubt! Then let's go the whole way and have her legs amputated by an amateur. Besides, it didn't hurt any less with a doctor, because there was no anesthetic in either case. Afterwards she was Peg-Leg Annie and went about without complaint on the stumps of her legs, doing washing for the miners who had once sought her favors and who paid her very well for the menial tasks she now performed.

Just the opposite of the bespectacled fact-finders who crave accuracy, though it cost a tale its point, are those wide-eyed young things combing the records for romantic tidbits, or professional fiction-writers glamorizing the Old West. These are the ones who will take a tale like that of Polly Bemis, the Chinese slave girl, and her lover, the tin-horn gambler of Warren, Idaho, who won her at a game of cards with her Chinese master, and blow it up into a fantasy half pioneer *Madame Butterfly*, half frontier Hemingway. This is the kind of romance that the first old hard-rocker will deflate without effort:

"Polly Bemis? Why, sure I remember her. Little old Chiny woman lived up the South Fork of the Salmon. Great pipe-smoker — opium. Was the woman of Charlie Bemis, the gambler. No, never heard he won her at cards. Well, mebbe she did nurse him through a shooting accident. Ever hear how he got his eye put out? Well, he was lyin' in front of the saloon in Warren one day and a fellow comes up and says to him: 'Bemis, if you don't pay me that money you owe me I'm a goin' to shoot your eye out.' Well, sir, Bemis was lyin' there with his hat over his face and he just pushed it back and looked at the fellow and says: 'Shoot!' and he shot. Yessir, Bemis had only one eye. Died years later. Died with only one eye."

People didn't mince words in those days. When a nameless woman came to a gold-strike in the Coeur d'Alenes with nineteen men and during an argument with one of them shot him dead with his own pistol, it was taken calmly. She simply stepped to the door of the tent and announced quietly: "I've shot Hardhat!" That's all there was to it. Good riddance, anyway. Hardhat, in all likelihood, would be missed by no one, not even his mother. A committee was set up to act as coroner. In the committee's report it was regretted that it had been left to a lady to clean up the camp.

Frontier justice was rugged and individualistic. No one thought any less — in fact, everyone thought rather better — of an old judge who liked to tell the story of how he was trying the case of a famous attempt at murder, and during the time of the trial he fell off his horse into an icy stream and had to put in at an empty cabin to dry himself off. He couldn't get a fire started without paper and finally he took the testimony out of his inside pocket, used it in the stove, and dismissed the case on the grounds of insufficient evidence. The case didn't have much point anyway, in his opinion. Nobody was hurt. The intended victim had been saved by the lump of silver dollars he carried in his pocket, which the bullet dented but did not penetrate. Main point of it was: "No ladies was hurt, so why not forget about it?" Men should be able to take care of themselves.

Women who frequented dance halls, hurdy-gurdy houses, and other social centers of mining-camp days were bound to see some fancy shooting and some fancy characters. The greatest marksman of them all was Hank Vaughn, who liked to whip out a silk handkerchief, give an end to an opponent, and shoot it out with him at handkerchief range. Ferd Patterson, another flashy gentleman, noted for his prowess at faro, was long remembered for his special get-up consisting of high-heeled shoes, plaid trousers, a watch-chain of nugget, and a frock coat of beaver trimmed with otter. When no one is left alive who can remember Ferd's costumes, Idaho records will remember him because he scalped his mistress.

Contrary to the written opinion of historians, old-timers assert that a dance-hall or hurdy-gurdy woman was not as good as the average woman in a parlor house. And again that qualifying adjective "good" applies not to their personal lives (which were not judged), but to their standards of fair play, generosity of spirit, and so on. Old-timers will tell you that hurdy-gurdy girls tried to get something for nothing. They would rob a man when he was off guard, and they charged high for such innocent pleasures as waltzing — sometimes a dollar a dance. Half of the dollar supposedly went to the management and half to the girl. This was a high rate and clearly indicates the scarcity of women and the value put upon them. A history of Idaho states that a large proportion of these girls were German and were engaged in sets of four — with a chaperon! "Chaperon!" yells an old-timer with a look compounded of scorn and full-bodied amusement. "Well, that's a new name for it."

The names of most dance-hall girls have been forgotten. One exception is Anna King, who was murdered in a dance-hall brawl at Bonanza and was buried by a committee of miners from Custer who learned that respectable townsfolk did not want her bones to lie in the town graveyard. They planted her well to one side in a square of earth marked by four pine trees. So magnificent were these trees that Anna's grave became eventually a state beauty spot cared for by the Department of Forestry.

There were rough times everywhere in the days when men made money in phenomenal spurts and had no way to spend it but on liquor and women. Yet landladies in well-known mining towns ran respectable houses and maintained law and order with a grim eye, a quick tongue, and the aid of a Chinaman who opened the door, cooked, tended bar, and kept accounts and secrets with equal passivity.

A good parlor house had an air of luxury and comfort which few private homes in frontier country possessed at the time. To get a piano over the mountains and up and down the rocky grades of mining country was in itself a feat of some magnitude. Parlor houses of the first class set a good table and prided themselves on their cellars. The women sent east for their finery or bought it from itinerant peddlers, and whatever plumes, feathers, silks, and lace stockings they could get together are still a

tender memory to men who were leading a life of almost inde-
scribable deprivation and roughness in the hope of striking it
rich in the hills. Crumbling and woebegone communities which
were once roarng bonanzas in the Idaho mountains still harbor
old characters who recall champagne suppers and singing in
the evening around a piano with "the girls — all dressed up
proper, you can bet. Better dressed than any women you saw
anywhere else, and wearing corsets too when they came downstairs. And no rough stuff. It wasn't allowed. And no rough
talk either." The most successful landladies maintained a strict
air of respectability and charming home-life, on the ground
floor at least.

There were also parlor houses and opium dens with Ori-
ental atmosphere to take care of the thousands of Chinamen
who poured into the mining country of the Pacific Northwest
in early boom days — often patiently to work the once-washed
claims of the whites. These Orientals set up their own community — a "Chinatown" — and lent their special life and color
to an otherwise drab and ugly place. There were Chinese
women, known by the dramatic name of "slave girls," who
appeared on gala occasions like Chinese New Year to dazzle
all beholders with their creamy beauty, the intricacy of their
hair ornaments, and the embroidery of their garments. They
rode quietly with downcast eyes in an open carriage among the
lanterns, firecrackers, skyrockets, colored umbrellas, and paper
kites of a typical Chinese holiday crowd.

Chinese women, when young and beautiful, often made a
powerful impression on the minds of young boys whose hard-
driven, overworked, unadorned pioneer mothers had little left
of any original charm or freshness they might have had before
trekking overland to the Idaho hills. An old judge, dreaming
among the carefully preserved records of one of Idaho's wild-
est towns — now a decaying stage-set for some nostalgic Western
movie — recalls the young bride of Old Wing Kee with an almost loverlike tenderness:

"We used to watch her comb her hair in the mornings. Old
Kee said we could, if we never got smart, or tried to sass her,

or made any noise. She'd take her long black hair and smooth it out over her ear — just like a bird's wing. Seems like she had some kind of paste she used, made of rhubarb — and she'd lay her hair along the side of her head, sort of fan-shape. It was neat as a pin and yet somehow, I dunno, it wasn't plain, it was fancy, or it seemed fancy. She wore silk trousers and an embroidered jacket and she had the tiniest feet you ever saw — tiny as a baby's. Her hands were tiny too, and white, with little fingers, and they folded in sort of, like a bird's claw, only not bony."

The Chinese introduced opium-smoking into Idaho towns, but it never took hold of the white populace. Men who remember as adventurous boys going into the "dives" and walking about among the sleeping occupants of the little private cells rarely recall the experience without a shudder. "It was different from drunks. With a drunk he was out, and you knew where he was. But with pipe-smokers, well, it was as though they had gone some place you or nobody could follow. They were really gone."

There was an established hierarchy of authority and social standing in all parlor-houses. The occupant of the lowest rung of the social ladder was the piano-player, known always as "the professor." The status of a professor was well below that of a pimp. A gentleman of the latter category was an habitué of a house who stood in a special relationship to one of the girls. This relationship permitted him to black her eye, beat her, and regularly take her hard-earned money with what amounted to legal rights. In the Far West only infrequently did a gentleman of this calling drum up trade for his mistress. Perhaps trade didn't need drumming up.

Why the piano-player was of such lowly status is difficult to determine, but all old-timers agree that he was. Sometimes he was blind. Sometimes he was the black sheep of a good family. Sometimes he was merely a young man trying to earn money to make his way in the world — but he never lived down such a dubious means of getting a start. Saloon-keepers and gamblers might — and in all likelihood would — rise in the world without difficulty and live to see their grandchildren occupying airy social summits, but not the piano-player. A well-known citizen in the Intermountain country who managed to become a respected member of local society earned the money that made him a lawyer by playing a piano in a parlor house. He found it such a dark cloud on his subsequent career that he was quoted as saying to a man about to marry: "If you ever have children, never let them learn to play the piano. It almost ruined me."

The pariah status of "professors" is made perfectly clear in a story told in Hailey, Idaho, by an old man with a young memory. The story concerns a Dutchman who returned to camp with a black eye and on questioning replied — with a Dutch accent guaranteed to bring down the house — "Vell, I vent to see that sveet Amy and I had a nize time, but ven in the morning I started uptown, the piano-player he valked along vith me and I said to him: 'It's better maybe you valk a little quicker as I don't vant to valk uptown mit a vhorehouse piano player,' and he hauled off and hit me in the eye."

Parlor house fights were more infrequent than you might believe, but they did take place. Sometimes the cause lay in the sudden striking it rich of a man in the hills who would come to the nearest town and take over a house until he had spent all his gold. He would bring his friends and fellow prospectors and they would eat, drink, dance, and celebrate until the last cent was gone. Then the landlady — invariably a generous-hearted old girl — would say: "The party's over, but here, take this, you'll be needing it," and she would give him some money to tide him over. Also she would grub-stake him for his return to the hills. While he was spending his money, however, the regular patrons of a house sometimes resented exclusion from their favorite haunts. They would then organize a gang of their friends and storm the citadel. Some Homeric combats took place as a consequence. One old man, well past seventy, on his way back to the hills for the hundredth time in a kaleidoscopic life, stopped long enough to recall one of the battles of his youth. His eyes gleamed and his false teeth beat a delicate castanet in pleasure as he described the high point of the fray in which he climbed up on the grand piano with the big brass spittoon in his hands the better to "klop" his assailant (whose back was fortunately turned at the moment as he reached for a chair) "on the noggin with the gaboon." The force of the blow broke the piano top, but he was glad to pay for it. After all, the sum was a minor figure in the days when men shook dice on the corner of the bar for a thousand dollars a throw.

The origins of most landladies and famous female characters of the mining boom days are lost forever. Any woman who got ahead and eventually ran her own place invariably had "folks back East who never knew nothing about her life until they came to bury her" — and sometimes not then, as the whole town would turn out to honor one of these women if she had been enough of a public benefactor. Such funerals quite often began solemnly and ended in carnival, which was probably quite in accordance with the wishes of the deceased. One famous character's last ride near Boise turned into a spirited horse race. The hearse and the carriages of the mourners on the way to the cemetery were driving abreast, rather than in a single line, in order to avoid the heavy fog of alkaline dust raised in dry weather. The parallel arrangement proved too much for the suggestible drivers. One man applied his whip. The rest followed suit. . . . The hearse won.

Stories which do survive of the origins of any of these women are never dull. That of Mother Mac of Silver City presents some special psychological overtones. She was a good woman and a model wife until the day when neighbors came bringing the news that her husband was dead in a mine accident. She took to her bed and the bottle — which she had never touched before — and remained alone, drinking, until she passed into a coma. "Never washed or combed her hair or nothing." When she emerged from the coma she put the bottle away and never touched it again. She packed her bags and departed for the booming town of Silver City, Idaho. Here she calmly opened the best parlor house in the community, although, it is asserted, she herself took no part in local revels and remained true to the memory of her husband.

Molly b'Damn is another personality whose mysterious origins tease the fancy. She appeared in the mining town of Murray in 1884 with a packtrain from Thompson's Falls. She had no name but Molly b'Damn. Her contemporaries describe her as "an uncommonly ravishing personality. Her face gave no evidence of dissipation, her clothes no hint of her profession. About her, at times, was an atmosphere of refinement and culture." On occasion "she quoted with apparent understanding from Shakespeare, from Milton, from Dante. She was soon the reigning queen of the Murray underworld." She died in her bed with the mystery about her still unsolved and the miners buried her in grand style in the lonely hills.

Another famous Idaho character whose respectable married name is best left unmentioned is said to have been a sister of Calamity Jane. This statement is sworn to by the ballad-singing, half-blind hermit who lives near the Golden Anchor mine alone with his memories, which include such garish items as a harem of seven Sioux squaws. This old man bases his assertion on his remembrance of the night he saw Calamity Jane's brother going down to a dance hall — whether in Deadwood Gulch, Blackfoot, or Virginia City he did not say — to shoot his younger sister because she was "turnin' out bad." Apparently the younger sister decided to leave home hastily, for she survived, and she did not reform. The records say that Calamity Jane — who could outlie, outshoot, outswear, and outdrink any ten men of her era, and who boasted of campaigning against the Arizona Apaches, scouting for Sioux on the Rosebud, and swimming the Platte River with dispatches for Custer, thus avoiding the massacre of the Little Big Horn — did have a sister. She had, as a matter of record, two, but data on them are scarce, ranging from virtuous deaths from tuberculosis brought on by leaning over steaming laundry tubs, to apprenticeship to Mother Mustache, the queen of the underworld gamblers of six states. The latter activity seems a more likely career for a sister of the Far West's most untrammeled female. This sister, if such she was, had another name before her Idaho one. It was, says the hermit of the Golden Anchor, Lousy Liz.

She came walking on foot, a woman no longer in her first youth, through the Idaho foothills in early spring, bound for the Thunder Mountain mining boom. In latter years she admitted, rather shamefacedly, that the beauty of the countryside in its spring green persuaded her to stay. She found a willing and lonesome old-timer who married her and she settled down to collecting furs, and weird gnarled roots which she had cut, polished, and made into furniture. By the time she died her collections of furs and furniture had become famous. Even in the solitude of the lonely Idaho hills drama was bound to seek out such a woman. One day three men came through her place bound for a prospecting site up on the mountain above her. She exchanged a few words with them and wished them luck. A week later one of them, nearly dead — and well past all help — came crawling on his belly into the yard. His companions were both gone, he said. They died the first night they opened their home-packed rations. He had managed to crawl out and down the mountain, but by the next day he too was dead. The woman had him buried on the hill behind her house. This was in autumn. In the spring, with the waters still swollen with melting snow, a tight-faced woman came asking her way to the destination of the three prospectors. The old hermit of the Golden Anchor, much younger then and not yet blind, led her to the abandoned camp, though it was hard going. She paid him well to dig up the bodies and look at the remains, and she stopped at the third grave on the hill before going away. The hermit is sure, as was Calamity Jane's sister, that it was she who had packed their poisoned food. She wanted to make certain that they were all quite dead. No one reported her. People minded their own business in those days. The assumption would be that she had her reasons for what she did. They concerned no one else. Certainly a relative of Calamity Jane's wasn't going out seeking the law.

"We used to be realists," said the former mayor of an Idaho

town. "Now we're ostriches. I always encouraged parlor houses. What else are you going to do in a frontier community with twenty men to every woman? I could tell the Army a thing or two about public health. . . . Another thing, competition makes for better conditions in the sporting world. One parlor house in a town is no good. When I had only one I telephoned to Boise and got an old Silver City girl on the phone. 'Mamie,' I said, 'come on over here and open up a place. I've got a good proposition for you.' She came and we made an agreement — no public advertising, no fights, regular medical examination. When the town got virtuous and closed the parlor houses I want you to know disease shot up in this place like a rocket."

"Times aren't so different," said an old Idahoan who had made and lost a series of fortunes in sheep, mining, and saloon-keeping. "I don't notice much general improvement. If any-thing, I think people are looser now — in a different way. I don't think people know as much about entertaining themselves any more either. I can remember the old days when the Basque sheep-herders used to come into my place up at the Forks and put on a special dance they had. No, not around a woman's hat on a pole — but I've heard about that one. This was different. They'd start dancing to someone playing one of them accor-dions they had, and they'd begin peeling off their clothes, first their hats, then their shirts, then their trousers, and so on down — all but their boots — they kept them on — and when they was all naked they'd start dressing again, all in time to the music and no rough stuff and no getting out of rhythm, and the last fellow dressed stood the drinks. Where'd you see a thing like that any more, I want to know? Except maybe in the movies — all sugared up for the public."

"People don't seem to have time for any fun any more," said another old-timer, looking out at the sunbaked hills with his rheumy blue eyes. "Maybe people haven't got the hearts they used to have. People used to be on the same level, seems to me. Now, take Silver City — life was rough, but everybody knew everybody. After I heard my father tell my mother the story

[135]

of Mother Mac I stopped dropping stones on her roof from the hill, like I used to. . . ." His voice went on, dreamily, nasally.

On the desk before him lay the *Historical Directory* of Owyhee County, Idaho, 1898. Where he had opened it there was a reproduction of a photograph showing a back-drop of a castle-like mansion, turreted and gabled, a cross between Spanish and Norman English. Before this dream-image there had been posed a work-worn frontier couple with sunken eyes, lined and hard-bitten faces. Said the book: "The social life of Silver City is free from the petty jealousies and heart-burnings that are so common in small places where the upper ten and codfish aristocracy swell over their inferiors. Here there is a pleasant natural commingling between all classes, and a cordial hospitality rules society."

The general attitude in mining country toward "sporting women" was straightforward and honest. Men felt genuine gratitude for their presence in a rough and ugly environment which had little externally to tempt a woman to stay. The most successful landladies were, judging from the oral records — and there are no others — hard-headed realists, forthright and outspoken, warm-hearted to a fault, generous to the sick and those down on their luck. Undoubtedly it was not merely a first fatal "slip," but a real appetite for life beyond the confines of some restricted Middle Western community that sent many of these women west on their great adventure.

VIII. The Prophet

WHEN NARCISSA WHITMAN and Eliza Spalding upset the estab·
lished routine of daily life at Fort Vancouver by taking their
meals with the men, instead of accepting the segregation to
which the Indian and half-breed wives at the fort were accustomed, they were unconsciously forecasting new conditions in
the Far Northwest. The young daughter of the chief factor
wrote of them with a certain wistfulness: "When the missionary ladies came it was quite different. Then we mingled more."
It has been pointed out that Narcissa and Eliza were, without
realizing it, the first local advocates of women's rights.

Women who had walked or ridden month after weary month
across desert and mountain, enduring all the hardships of the
men, and running greater risks because of their physical handi-
caps, were not of a mind to be excluded from any masculine
privileges once they reached the Far West. Mrs. Whitman was
considerably piqued when certain members of the missionary
band objected to women praying aloud in public in the company of men. Had she been alive forty years later when Abigail Scott Duniway was using church platforms from which
to speak of the subject of women's rights, it is likely that Narcissa would have lent her enthusiastic support.

Abigail Scott, who was to become Abigail Duniway — one
of the most reviled and eventually one of the most honored
of Far Western women — was only a young girl when, in 1851,
she made the long trip to Oregon with her family. As an old
woman, writing the tart and tender reminiscences of her long
fight for equal suffrage, she said she could look back to childhood and see already hints of the kind of woman she was to
become. When still just a child, during the dramatic "log cabin
and hard cider" campaign of William Henry Harrison, she
stood on a stump in an Illinois village to harangue her play-
mates about "Tippecanoe and Tyler too." Words were to be
her tools.

Abigail was seventeen when the Scott family — over the ineffectual protests of the mother — set out on the journey to the West. It was Abigail who kept the journal of the plains trip, though the task might well have fallen to her talented brother, Harvey, destined to become in time the great editor of the Northwest's first great newspaper, the *Oregonian*.

Abigail was by nature ambitious, quick-witted, passionate, and studious. Though nothing was supposed to be taken on the trail to Oregon worth less than a dollar a pound, serious-minded Abigail managed to smuggle into the covered wagon Webster's *Elementary Speller*. She was eager for knowledge and for experience, but young in life she faced the hard truth that to be a woman was a severe handicap. She could always remember with bitter irony the weeping words of her mother at the birth of a new child: "Poor baby! She'll be a woman some day. Poor baby! A woman's lot is so hard." No one wanted girls on the Midwestern frontier, though it was to be different later in the Far West, where women were at a premium.

Abigail, the third child born in less than four years to a frail woman, was the second girl of the family. The first-born, a boy, had died. When she was only ten, Abigail heard from her mother the story of the disappointment she had felt at the arrival of a second daughter. Abigail never forgot this painful blow to her pride. It started her questioning woman's lot in the world. She herself was to have five sons and one daughter, and — perhaps in consequence of her own early hurt — the daughter always held the place closest to her heart.

Mrs. Scott died on the Western trip, succumbing easily to cholera, worn out as she was with years of drudgery and constant childbearing. All her sensitive children suffered from this loss, but none more than Abigail, unless it was Harvey, who as a grown man would pace the floor in the nights, still tortured with thoughts of the essential tragedy of his mother's life. When Abigail was waging her great suffrage fight in the Western country, her brother, without openly espousing the suffrage cause, would insert in his powerful newspaper helpful stories of injustice to women. Thus he tried to balance the sorry ledger.

In spite of Abigail's native gifts of intelligence and spirit, fate might well have kept her bitter and frustrated in anonymous drudgery on some Oregon farm had not a series of misfortunes paradoxically provided her with a way out. Shortly after reaching Oregon, she married Ben Duniway and gave up school-teaching to become, like all women of the period, a "servant without wages." Her days followed a monotonous, heavy round of scrubbing, washing, churning, milking, mending, sewing, and cooking not only for her family and the hired men, but for assorted bachelor friends of Mr. Duniway's who frequented the Duniway "hotel" as Abigail called it.

Abigail's powerful will gave her a seemingly inexhaustible source of energy. Actually she was not a strong woman and she said in after years — with the bitterness that she could not keep from her remembrances — that she was poorly fitted for the tasks she, as a farmer's wife, was expected to perform for "hale and hearty men." Her physical weakness was due to the fact that her "faithful mother" had worn both herself and Abigail "to a frazzle" by similar drudgery before Abigail was born.

Her first chance to escape farm toil came when her husband, without consulting her or asking her advice — indeed, against her unsolicited protest — signed a note for a friend. What Abigail had feared would happen shortly came to pass. Mr. Duniway was forced to pay the note and thereby lost his farm. This incident gave Abigail her first close look at a grave social injustice. Although she, as a woman, had nothing to say about the disposal of their property, when the summons was served in the absence of her husband, it was legally served on her. What kind of law was this? You were held jointly accountable with your husband, yet you had no rights of your own?

Enraged as she was by this example of woman's inequality before the law, Abigail was secretly pleased by the loss of the farm. It allowed the Duniways to move to town. In town the second fateful yet fortunate mischance occurred: her husband was invalided in a runaway accident. To most women the future would now have looked very dark. The prospect of supporting a family single-handed might have broken a weaker spirit, but to Abigail it pointed the way to eventual freedom. She got a job teaching school. Although she had to rise at three in summer and four in winter to clean house and prepare breakfast for her six children, her husband, and her boarders, she did not mind. She could at least "rest" at her desk while teaching the primary classes. With the upper divisions, however, there was little rest. She never had time to study any of the lessons in advance and had to work them out with her unsuspecting pupils as they went along. But she was learning with them, and this was reward enough for her.

School-teaching was to Abigail simply a means to earn enough money to go into a trade where she might really prosper. She was always fundamentally a realist. Although she considered education of paramount concern, she knew that educators were never honored with more than a living wage. Abigail had plans and they involved the making of money. As soon as she had thirty painfully saved dollars in her pocket, she went to Portland to interview the town's richest merchant, Jacob Meier. She wanted to start a millinery and notions store in Albany. Some idea of Abigail's air of determination and efficiency can be gained from the fact that Meier insisted that she take $1,200 worth of goods on credit. Abigail was persuaded to plunge and did so. In three weeks she was back with her debts paid, willing to risk $3,000 more.

Millinery led Abigail into life. She had an opportunity to observe, at first hand, contemporary females from every walk of life. What she saw did not impress her. Including herself in her judgment, she remarked that "half of us are dolls, half of us are drudges, and all of us are fools."

Abigail, honest and forthright to a fault, had to share indirectly in the little games of deceit which women — given no allowance and no financial independence — had to practice on their husbands. She would see women pretend to buy for their little girls, in the presence of their husbands, the "six-bit" hats favored by Indian berry-pickers, and, the moment the man left the store, change to the fashionable "Neapolitans." The difference in price they paid off bit by bit as they could pilfer small change from their husbands' pockets in the nights.

When Abigail, troubled at being an accomplice in dishonesty, took her misgivings to another merchant of Albany, he only laughed at her qualms. Said he: "We merchants couldn't make any profit on fancy goods if it wasn't for what the women steal from their husbands."

But Abigail could not condemn women alone. Husbands stole too. They stole the "butter money" of their wives — the one pitiful source of income allowed to women in a farming countryside. Among all the sordid tales she heard of stolen butter money the one that rankled longest had to do with a prosperous farmer who took his wife's careful hoard and contributed it to the purchase of a thoroughbred racehorse that was the talk of the countryside. The poor woman, far gone in illness, with a flock of little stair-steps, a babe at her breast, and another on the way, came to Abigail to beg a job of plain sewing to enable her to buy her disappointed little girls the waterproof suits she had been promising them for a year. Before the next year was out the woman was dead, and Abigail, listening to a minister preach a sermon of condolence to the bereaved husband, felt the juices of anger and discontent stir strongly in her heart.

It was all too plain that women had no rights of any kind. Abigail — the confidante of the countryside — could not keep out of the little dramas enacted around her daily. She would go with weeping women to court to protest injustices. She would try to set up in a boarding house, or in some small business, a wife and mother whose drunkard husband had deserted her — only to have the husband return and again drink up the savings and mortgage anew the furniture.

Abigail sowed the seeds of question in as many feminine minds as she dared. Even before she broke all precedent and went out into public life with her challenge to women to assert their rights, she had a foretaste of the pillorying to which she was to be subjected.

The first sign of community disapproval came in a valentine, of which Abigail was able to speak with amusement in her old age, though at the time it brought only floods of tears. The valentine showed the picture of a trembling henpecked husband to whom squalling children were clinging, while an ugly witch of a woman brandished a broom. Below were written the words:

> Fiend, devil's imp, or what you will
> You surely your poor man will kill,
> With luckless days and sleepless nights,
> Haranguing him with Woman's Rights.

Actually it was her caricatured husband to whom Abigail gave credit for showing her that though she might protest all she pleased about the slavery of women, nothing would change until females had the right to vote and equal rights before the law. The "light broke" on her, as she said, at the age of thirty-six. She then deliberately chose woman suffrage for her life work, taking Lincoln's words about equality for all "and by no means excluding women" as her watchword.

In 1871 Abigail moved her family to Portland and founded a newspaper for women, the *New Northwest*. Portland was only a village with one main street of shops, a few crude hotels and Chinese laundries, with saloons along the river-front, but it was the leading community of the state. She rented two upper bedrooms of a two-story frame house, hired a foreman at twenty-five dollars a week, set her sons to learning printing, and was soon well embarked on the next stage of her career.

The founding of a newspaper for women was an astounding feat. It put her at once into the same category with such brave women of the East as Susan B. Anthony, Julia Ward Howe, Elizabeth Cady Stanton, who, since the Civil War, had determined to gain for themselves privileges no longer denied "even the meanest ex-slave."

In the same year that she founded her newspaper Abigail

met for the first time the great Susan B. Anthony. She came to Portland to speak on woman suffrage, and Abigail, as her manager, toured the Willamette Valley towns and went north into Washington Territory to spread the word. The *New Northwest,* as the channel for information about the notorious visiting "man-hater," found its circulation booming. Foe as well as friend took to reading it.

Her years as a milliner had helped Abigail to understand the psychology of women. She knew that you often reached them through such frivolous or seemingly unimportant matters as hem-lengths, recipes for mutton stew, ideas on cutting over an old moire. So she began a free-advice-to-readers column in her newspaper. It abounded in homely advice, but it also conveyed in pithy style her opinions on matters essentially feminine.

She interested herself in fashions: "You need not make a skirt with a train. Hope you are going to be a sensible help-meet to your future husband and, if so, you must begin by dressing sensibly. A trailing dress is an emblem of degradation."

Abigail looked forward to the day when a woman could "go to a fashionable clothier's, get a suit of clothes as a man now can and have done with this eternal nonsense about something suitable to wear."

Women responded to the new newspaper. They wrote asking desperately what they could do to earn a living, naming their pitiful qualifications. Abigail would fire back suggestions. To one eager woman she wrote suggesting that the correspondent open a shirt factory: "We could assist you to buy linen, muslin, buttons and thread at wholesale prices and can give you exact patterns of the most celebrated styles."

Once, astonishingly enough, she suggested: "Why couldn't you open an intelligence office?" It would be interesting to know what qualifications this particular woman had sent in.

Occasionally Abigail's public correspondence gives a psychological insight into one of the darker convolutions of her nature: "No, we don't believe in bridal tours. Spend your honeymoon with your bereaved mother whose present heartache you will never realize until your daughter stands in your present situation." A honeymoon with a mother-in-law! What kind of woman was this? Abigail's autobiography, *Path Breaking,* and the columns of her paper reveal that where her daughter was concerned, she was a woman with a most possessive nature. Clara was the great love of her life. Abigail confessed in a chapter of her book called *Mortuary Reminiscences* that when Clara died she too wished to die, but her daughter murmured, "You must stay to finish your work, Ma." Abigail had hoped that Clara would continue where she left off, but this was not to be. Seemingly quite out of character, yet very revealing, is her further comment on Clara's death: "She passed away in January 1886, but I heard from her through private psychic sources within a month, and I have never since been able to think of her as dead."

The continued stories that Abigail wrote for her newspaper, *Ellen Dowd, the Farmer's Wife, Judith Reid, the Plain Story of a Plain Woman,* are clearly chronicles of her own experiences as a struggling young housewife and mother. Though they are hastily written, rambling, opinionated chronicles of the lives of women of the period, they undoubtedly attracted readers, for they told of the daily experiences common to the whole pioneer countryside.

Abigail's gift for homely narrative, her natural sense of the weight and use of words, were helpful to her when she began her public life as a speaker on the antagonizing subject of women's rights. Such a thing as a woman speaker was almost unheard of at that time. Abigail herself, not many years before, had been hissed for daring to enter a hall with her husband just to listen to a male lecturer. Though people might come to hear her for all the wrong reasons, Abigail did not mind. As long as she could raise her voice and be heard she would endure the physical hardships and the insults. And so she junketed through the Western states for years, enduring all the travel discomforts of the pioneer period and risking the loss of her good name by being forced to spend so much time in steamers and stagecoaches in the company of men only. With her strong handsome face alert under its conservative but expensive hat, with her "sensible" shoes, her neat gloves, her inevitable umbrella, she became a familiar figure to the captains of river steamboats and the drivers of stagecoaches in the expanding Western land.

In the red plush salons of the comfortable steamers that made the journey up the Columbia River to the inland country, Abigail planted her little seeds of rebellion in the minds of any women met by chance. If allowed to, she would make speeches on deck in those sections of the river between rapids when travelers were bored or restless. Under the rocky green cliffs of the western stretch of the river, or the stripped yellow hills of the eastern part, she would quietly take up collections for the cause. When the steamer tied up at some riverside village for the night, she would go ashore, try to find a room large enough to hold a meeting, and proceed to deliver a speech.

She endured uncomplainingly the hard journeys over roads that were virtually impassable in the long rainy season. She hoped only for the luck of a seat beside the driver, on the "boot" above the billows of dust. She was never too tired to enjoy local color and to store it away for a fund of homely incident on which she could draw in her speeches. She was one of the first women to brave the hazardous journey on Dorsey Baker's rawhide railroad from Wallula to Walla Walla. The trip was dangerous because cattlemen, fearing the end of the Western stage industry, blocked the doctor's enterprise in every way they could. Dead cattle across the tracks were a favorite device, but the pioneer capitalist foiled his enemies by training a little dog to run ahead on the tracks and give warning in time to avoid wrecks. After a day of stopping and starting, of jolting and swaying on the narrow-gauge track, Abigail would get off at Walla Walla, find a room, make herself tidy, and repair to the parlors of the Stein House to spread the word of equal suffrage.

She became used in time to being turned out of parlors by irate husbands when she was found deep in dangerous conversation with their timidly questioning wives. Yet many women as well as men hated and feared her. In Jacksonville, Oregon, she had the terrifying experience of being rotten-egged by some of the rough element in this mining town. "Missouri bush-whackers," Abigail called them, and referred to their weapons as "Jacksonville arguments."

No matter how much of a freak she was considered, the Pixley Sisters with their daring song-and-dance act could still get the hall of any town sooner than Abigail could. Clergymen, inclined to be lenient to a respectable woman with a message about "freedom," sometimes opened their churches to her, but few would attend who did not belong to the denomination the building served. Even in churches she was not free of the threat of heckling. Once a choir of women was organized to sing her down, and they would rise and burst into a hymn every time she got to her feet to speak. Finally they had to resort to the Doxology to clear the church, for Abigail just kept on rising and getting out a sentence at a time.

Sometimes in the fast-growing crude West her audience gathered in the skeleton frame of a future school, store, or hotel. Sometimes it was a blacksmith shop or a stable. Abigail even learned to accept the back room of a saloon on those occasions when the key of the hall she had engaged would be mysteriously missing. At least in the back room of a saloon she was sure of an audience — and an audience was all she wanted. By the yellow light of the kerosene lamps she would stand in quiet dignity, making her vivid pictures of women's daily humiliations, of the injustice implicit in the fact that those who bore the children had no legal right to decide anything about their lives; that an irresponsible drunkard could still, in the eyes of the law, take his wife's property for his own and impoverish his family without legal rebuke.

She knew how to make people laugh with her sharp retorts and the sting of her provincial wit. And often reluctantly they had to admire her for her spunk. Once the floor of a primitive half-constructed hotel collapsed with her audience, but Abigail's clear voice kept down panic: "Don't hurry, friends. Remain perfectly quiet and there will be no danger." Fortunately the lamps had not fallen from their brackets. The crowd obeyed Abigail's orders. Within half an hour they had gathered around her in another room.

Often after a lecture she had to sleep with children in a corner bed in some strange house. Frequently she sat up all night because there was no place for her to go, or because she had to travel after dark to make her next engagement.

Only "sporting" women lived life with such license as this, and Abigail paid a price for her courage. She heard many a libelous tale about herself — that she smoked, drank, met strange men in hotel bedrooms; that her husband was a broken man, that her children ran wild. Once a particularly scurrilous item was published about her in a Portland weekly. It came under the eyes of her loyal sons at the breakfast table. Rising and leaving their meal untouched, they went quickly from the house. Later in the day Abigail learned that they were out of jail on ten thousand dollars' bail, charged with assault and battery. When the next morning, in distress and trying to hold back her tears, she appeared on the main street of Portland to go about her business, a prominent young attorney, J. N. Dolph, who was later to be a Senator, came up to her and warmly extended his hand. A group of men, gathered in an excited knot to discuss the affair, promptly took their cue from Mr. Dolph. They ceremoniously removed their hats and remained uncovered as Abigail went weeping by. The community took the stand that the boys had done right to fight for their mother's good name. Even the prosecuting attorney, Judge J. F. Caples, risked his official standing to say to Abigail's boys: "Stay with it! You did exactly right!" Portland knew that Harvey Scott's sister might be a fire-eater but she was eminently respectable and the mother of five "good" sons.

Frequently when Abigail grew despondent over attacks her sense of humor saved her. Sometimes, however, her "dander" got the better of her. Once on arriving at a meeting she heard that a temperance speaker, annoyed at her refusal to link equal suffrage and prohibition, had accused her in public of indulging in "Bacchanalian revelries" with men in hotels. As soon as she heard this she sent a note to the platform asking the man to repeat what he had said before her arrival. After a whispered colloquy the assistant chairman rose to make a resolution that no one should be allowed to speak who was not already on the platform. They knew Abigail, but not quite well enough. She managed to get to her feet well up front and repeat what she had heard and to ask the man how he would like it if she took the opportunity of repeating "the often circulated scandal, falsely accusing him of killing four of his deceased wives." The meeting broke up.

Abigail's difference of opinion with the temperance forces led her into many difficulties. Actually it was one proof of her good common sense. She realized that women must not confuse their inalienable rights as human beings with a plea for protection from drunkards by compulsory prohibition. She saw that an idea about freedom, like the idea involved in equal suffrage, and an idea about prohibition by force, as involved in the campaign to deprive everyone — temperate as well as intemperate — of alcohol, were not ideas that could make a working team if linked together. Force and freedom were polar opposites no matter how you looked at the problem.

She believed that when the national officers of equal suffrage allied themselves with the group working for enforced temperance, hoping thereby to bring more women into their battle for votes, they disastrously retarded the progress of the suffrage movement. Those Western states that granted equal suffrage relatively early in the fight were states in which fanatic members of the W.C.T.U. were well outnumbered by ladies of more doubtful character but sounder knowledge of men. Idaho, Colorado, Wyoming, and Utah granted women the franchise with comparatively slight struggle — though Abigail made a hasty trip to Boise in 1896 to prevent the Women's Christian Temperance Union from "spoiling everything" with anti-saloon propaganda in a state composed largely of miners and cattlemen. In the four states that granted the franchise, Abigail remarked acidly that men had not been aroused to stubbornness by any "tambourine campaign." Washington, which had granted women the right to vote when it was still a territory, took away the privilege when it became a state, simply because, said Abigail, too many earnest and ill-advised females thought to get their way with a whip.

About the problem of liquor-drinking Abigail was hard-headed and dignified. She had talked too long about individual human liberty to allow herself the inconsistency of making an exception of those who enjoyed alcoholic spirits. The spectacle of pious women of certain Oregon communities taking their knitting and going to sit all day in local saloons as a way of shaming men out of drink made no appeal to her. She might even have sympathized — on the grounds of independent action for all — with the scene made by one harassed drinker in an Oregon saloon. After females had pushed their way into his favorite hang-out and annoyed him with their shrill hymn-singing and exhortations to seek Jesus, he turned around glass in hand to remark: *"This is my Christ!"* While the women stood gasping, he downed his whisky in a single gulp.

When an emotional and muddle-headed woman whom Abigail met on a train told her that it would not be long until that "curse of curses" alcohol would be driven from the land, Abigail tartly commented that in her opinion there was only one Power capable of prohibiting "snow-storms and alcohol" and He didn't seem ready to act. This piece of blasphemy led directly to the shocked question: "Do you mean to say that God is the author of alcohol?" "Certainly," responded Abigail. "The Bible tells us that God makes everything.'

Although Abigail did not believe in drink, never touched it, and had five sons who also were teetotalers, she had no patience with people who thought they could determine conduct for all their fellow men. Unctuous self-righteousness aroused her most bitter scorn. At a temperance meeting in Salem — in the early days before she saw clearly that the prohibition forces were going to wreak havoc with the equal-suffrage campaign — she had a run-in with a certain clergyman who said in a public speech: "I charge the sins of the world upon the mothers of men. There are twenty-two thousand fallen women in New York — two millions of them in America — we cannot afford to let this element vote."

Abigail jumped to her feet to retort. Shaking her finger menacingly at a minister who could utter such un-Christian words, she cried: "How dare you make such charges against the mothers of men? You tell us of two millions of fallen women, who, you say, would vote for drunkenness; but what say you, sir, to the twenty millions of fallen men — and all voters — whose patronage alone enables fallen women to live? Would you disfranchise *them,* sir? I pronounce your charge a libel on womanhood and I know that if we were voters you would not dare to utter it."

Abigail never lacked for a hot retort to pierce the balloons of prejudice and ignorance. One of the most common questions put to timid women who thought they might like to vote was: How would you like to serve on a jury and be locked in a room with eleven men? The idea was indecent. Indecent! cried Abigail; was it more indecent than the idea that, though women might not sit on juries, juries might try them for their lives? Another standard argument was that if women voted they should also fight. When it came to bravery, replied Abigail, what man in battle had ever faced more danger and pain than a woman during the delivery of a child. When a "conceited stripling," as she characterized him, remarked that he was willing to give women all their rights except the privilege of voting, she inquired smartly: "How did our rights and privileges, political or otherwise, happen to come into your possession, my boy?"

Abigail despised the use of such blinds as the words "supported" and "protected" which men so often applied to their wives. "Supported and protected at hard labor in an economical fashion," said she. Once riding on a stagecoach in eastern Washington — the only woman among men, as she so often was — a fellow traveller who had been warming himself with a bottle spoke up jocosely: "Madame! You ought to be at home enjoying yourself like my wife is doing. I want to bear all the hardships of life myself, and let her sit by the fire, toasting her footsies."

Abigail said nothing. Having no ammunition, she allowed the passengers to poke their elbows into one another's ribs at her expense. But, unhappily for the poor man, when the stage-coach dropped him in front of his isolated home, his wife stood in the yard in the falling snow chopping away at the wood-pile. "Good-by," cried Abigail, leaning out, "I see that your wife is toasting her footsies." She could still chuckle at that one in her seventies.

"The wonder was," said Abigail as an old woman, "that any-one should have been endowed with sufficient courage to en-dure and persevere in her demand for woman's enfranchise-ment."

But it didn't matter who it was, a stubborn butcher in Yakima or the great Horace Greeley, Abigail would not stand for any pompous nonsense. She met Horace Greeley on one of her many trips to the East to attend suffrage conventions. Gree-ley was running for president at the time and he received her cordially because he had been informed that she had made a speech warmly in his favor. But when Abigail spoke of her mission — which was to seek his endorsement of the suffrage movement — he irritably stroked his much caricatured whiskers and said in a voice "as hard as hailstones": "I don't want women to be men."

"Neither do I," responded Abigail, getting at once to her feet to leave. "I wouldn't be a man if I could! And now, Mr. Greeley, mark my words; you'll never be President. You will find that women can tear down, if they are not permitted to build up."

On the whole Abigail did not believe in threatening men. She never lost sight of the main point in dealing with them, which was that they alone enjoyed the privilege of voting, and that they alone had the power to grant women the same right. When Washington withdrew the franchise for women, she ap-proved of the subtle plan of Abbie H. H. Stuart of Olympia, who decided to draw women into the suffrage fold without their knowledge by interesting them in "culture." She founded the Olympia Women's Club, the progenitor of all Northwest women's clubs. In these clubs women, without alarming their husbands or even fully realizing themselves what was happening to them, prepared themselves for public life by learning how to conduct a meeting, how to address a chair, how to offer a motion, how to abide by rules of order.

This was just a little more subtle — and a somewhat more dignified — means of getting what they wanted than the tactics employed by other Washington suffragists. Mary Olney Brown described in the *History of Women Suffrage in America* the coups and compromises of the women of the territory of Washington, in the days when they had the right to vote but were laughed at for trying to exercise their franchise. On election day ladies who wanted to go to the polls organized elaborate picnic lunches. They played the old trick of lulling men's suspicions and lowering their resistance with fried chicken, hot biscuits, three-layer cakes, and then going on with them to the voting place — jovially indulged by their well-fed masters in their comic wish to play at being men. When less guileful women came along, however, and tried to threaten men with beerless picnics and whiskyless banquets, the husbands decided not to indulge their womenfolk any longer. They took back the franchise in 1887 and Washington women had to wait until 1910 to enjoy the vote again.

Oregon waited even longer. It was 1912 before Abigail Duniway, by now an old woman, signed the Equal Suffrage Proclamation of the state of Oregon. She had written the proclamation herself — an event as significant in the long unrecorded history of women as the writing of the Constitution of the United States was to humanity in general. For no woman had ever been entrusted with the framing of so important a paper. But the proclamation was inexcusably tardy in a state that over fifty years before had granted a woman's right to ownership of land in her own name, and as far back as 1874 a Married Woman's Property Bill to allow a married woman the rights to her own business if she had one. Abigail always blamed the delay on prohibitionists and meddling female outsiders from the national suffrage organization.

By the time Abigail died, in 1915, she had seen many changes. Women had come a long way from the status they enjoyed in 1876 when she — a keen-eyed young woman from the Far West — visited the Women's Pavilion at the Philadelphia Centennial and found there no objects more significant than "a few dresses sacred to royalty . . . the baby cap worn by John Quincy Adams, Jr.," and similar dull and ill-assorted oddments. Why not a faded calico dress and sunbonnet, a pair of homely shoes worn thin by tramping through the dust and stones of the American continent — so Abigail, the pioneer, might well have wondered.

In 1896, influenced by Mrs. Stuart's success with club meetings in Washington, Abigail organized a great congress of women in Oregon. Delegates were invited to consider the problems specifically related to women's world. Raised to the dignity of important matters were the care of children and the duties of motherhood. Medicine, education, art, science, literature, were seriously discussed, though all controversial subjects dealing with "sectarian gospels, partisan politics and political revolutions" were avoided. Susan B. Anthony lent the charm and force of her remarkable presence and Abigail could well look back on the conference with pride.

Right up to her last days Abigail was reminding women of the gratitude they should feel for the hard fight that certain indomitable females had made in their behalf. But when a reporter interviewed her, two days after it was certain that the suffrage amendment had passed in Oregon, she wanted to talk about the future, not about the past. It was only three years before her death, and she was an old lady in a cap and fichu, but she said she wanted to form right away a men's and women's Good Government Union. "I nearly said League," she told the reporter, "but so many people have asked me to keep out all such words as club, league or society, as it would seem to bar someone or other. This is what we want to avoid. We desire a Federated Union, non-partisan in every way. Our aim will be to work for what is best in government, sanitation, roads, child labor, and above all for rational recreation."

One of Abigail's last injunctions to women to remember the price that was paid for their freedom contains some of her noblest words:

"The young women of today, free to study, to speak, to write, to choose their occupation, should remember that every inch of this freedom was bought for them at a great price. It is for them to show their gratitude by helping onward the reforms of their own times, by spreading the light of freedom and of truth still wider."

And we know that Abigail is to be judged finally, not merely as a sharp-tongued feminist, but as a wise prophet when she can address to women this great and simple truth: "The debt that each generation owes to the past it must pay to the future."

IX. The Rebel

IN THE 1870's the town of Roseburg, Oregon, had been afflicted for some time with a public charge, an old pauper with a complication of diseases. This derelict had visited in turn every medical man of the community, and upon his death the doctors decided to get together and hold an autopsy to determine the sources of his singular ailments.

Although in the past, in small Western communities, an autopsy was often a semi-public event, a sort of ghoulish strip-tease — for men only — this particular autopsy would, in all likelihood, have passed unmarked in local history had it not been for the unseemly and scandalous role played in it by Bethenia Owens. Bethenia was a former milliner who not long before had shocked everyone she knew, alienated her friends, and embarrassed her family by traipsing off across country to the Philadelphia Eclectic College to get a medical degree at the only institution that would admit women to such unwomanly pursuits.

Her return from the East coincided with the performing of the autopsy on Roseburg's leading pauper. As the six doctors gathered in the shed on the outskirts of town to perform the operation before an audience of some fifty men and boys, one of them was seized suddenly with the brilliant idea of sending a mock invitation to the "Philadelphia doctor."

When Bethenia received the note, there is little doubt that she understood the intention behind it, and all the consequences that acceptance on her part would entail. But she did not hesitate for a moment. "Give the doctors my compliments," she said formally to the boy who delivered the invitation, "and say that I will be there in a few moments."

She reached the shed on the heels of the derisive laughter with which her answer was received. Opening the door with perfect dramatic timing, she walked straight up to the nearest physician and extended her hand. Out of the abrupt and shocked silence that greeted her appearance the doctor to whom she first addressed herself managed to mumble something in a low voice. Was Bethenia aware that this particular operation involved the genitalia? She was not, replied Bethenia, standing her ground, five feet four and every inch imperious. But, said she, looking in turn into their shifting eyes, to a doctor one part of the human body is as impersonal and as sacred as another.

In the fresh silence one of the outraged men — a doctor whom Bethenia had once put in his place because of his clumsy handling of a sick child — announced flatly that he objected to the presence of a woman at a male autopsy. If she were allowed to remain he would certainly leave.

Bethenia replied promptly. "I came here," she said as coolly as she could manage, "by formal invitation, and I will leave it to a vote whether I go or stay. But first I would like to ask Dr. Palmer what is the difference between the attendance of a woman at a male autopsy, and the attendance of a man at a female autopsy."

No one, including Dr. Palmer, had a ready reply, and the doctor with whom she had first shaken hands on entering the shed finally remarked that since he had suggested that she be invited he would vote for her to remain. Four other doctors reluctantly agreed. In the end Dr. Palmer alone angrily retired.

The assembled company then turned their attention to the corpse. The pauper was lying on boards supported by sawbucks, covered with an old worn gray blanket. As one of the doctors opened a medicine case containing the instruments for the operation, the interest of the fifty men and boys in the audience picked up. To Bethenia's shocked dismay, the doctor with the medicine case handed it across to her without a word. She had hardly bargained for this, and for a moment she was too stunned to speak. When she did, it was only to ask faintly: "You don't want me to do the work, do you?"

"Oh yes, yes," he said with feigned indifference. "Go ahead!"

There was absolute silence in the close-packed shed while the men waited, watching her. Bethenia did not hesitate long.

She resolutely took the instruments from him and began the operation.

As she operated, the word flew up and down the streets of the little town about what was happening in the old shed on the outskirts. If Bethenia believed that the men who were present secretly applauded her pluck and skill, she could hardly have been prepared for the reception she was to get when she emerged. She left the shed pale, shaken, but inwardly triumphant. She found the streets outside full of women and children who had come to laugh and catcall, to point their fingers, and titter behind their hands. Blinds were drawn, doors were slammed as there walked past them an ex-milliner who had dared to officiate at so disgusting a spectacle.

The whole town rocked with the incident. Had it not been for the well-known and respected trigger eye of Dr. Bethenia's brothers, Flem and Josiah — who, though shamed to the quick by their sister's act, would allow no indignities to be visited upon her — she might have had a very bad time of it. Perhaps Flem remembered the day in childhood when he had knocked off a piece of her front tooth while wrestling with her over who should go to the barn for a bundle of oats. Perhaps he remembered how he had run off crying bitterly. Whatever the reason for the loyalty, Bethenia, writing her memoirs many years later, was willing to concede that her family name and pioneer connections in the Umpqua River countryside undoubtedly saved her from being tarred and feathered and run out of town. She knew that only a short time before, women medical students leaving a hospital in more advanced Philadelphia had been publicly rotten-egged by their male fellow students.

After all, this was a period when men in places like the United States Congress rose to say: "We don't want our wives and daughters to be mathematicians, philosophers or scientists. We don't love and honor them for what they know of such things, but rather for what they don't know."

Bethenia, a long-time champion of the rights of women, understood her position in Roseburg, Oregon, only too well.

There was just one course open to her: to leave town as quickly and as quietly as possible. She did so, taking with her to more cosmopolitan Portland her degree from the Philadelphia Eclectic College. There she set up offices in which she could give electric and medicated baths as a part of the limited practice open to her as a female doctor.

The story of how Bethenia Owens came to the place where she had not only the courage but the knowledge to perform an autopsy, and subsequently to become the Far West's first graduate woman physician, is a long tale of spunk and rebellion.

Courage was nothing new in Bethenia's family line. One of her grandfathers had been an Indian-fighter, a scout and spy who received from the government for conspicuous bravery — in a time when all men were brave of necessity — a "silver-mounted rifle worth three hundred dollars." The Owens family came through to Oregon in the famous emigration of 1843. This was the notable band of pioneers led by Jesse Applegate, one of Oregon's wise men, later to be known as the "Sage of Yoncalla." Applegate was captain of the train, and Bethenia's father was captain of the buffalo-hunters.

The Owens party had the honor of being met at Independence Rock and guided through the Rocky Mountains by Dr. Marcus Whitman, the missionary martyr. Bethenia, though only a young child, could remember the great doctor, and other heroes and characters of the trail and mountain such as Peg-Leg Smith, whom they saw on the Snake River with his harem of squaws, "representing quite a tribe " in themselves.

Bethenia's early life and antecedents did not lack for color. Her father she described as a "tall athletic Kentuckian" who had been made a sheriff's deputy at the ripe age of sixteen. Of him people were wont to say: "Thomas Owens is not afraid of man or devil." The same might well have been said of his daughter, Bethenia. She was so adept at all boyish sports that her father often patted her on the head and called her his boy — not for lack of sons, certainly, since the Owens family, in true pioneer style, welcomed a new baby every two years. But

Bethenia liked to do what her brothers did and always remembered the year of the Whitman massacre because it was the year she won a bet with one of them that she could carry two hundred pounds of flour.

Little, tough, yet delicate, Bethenia, with her high spirits and her sensitive nature, was destined like many girls of her time — and, for that matter, of all times — to make an unfortunate first marriage. She was just fourteen and still very much a tomboy when she married Legrand Hill and went to keep house for him in a log hut she chinked herself with grass and mud against the snakes and lizards.

She had three years of marriage with an idler who proved more interested in "going to camp meetings . . . and hunting" than in getting any work done or providing for their future. Divorces in those days were not easily come by. Flagrant adultery was the only Biblical justification and it had to be pretty flagrant. When Bethenia came home to say that she didn't know whether she could stick the course or not, her tough-fibered pioneer father broke down and cried, but her mother was only indignant at a young husband who could not make a go of things in spite of all his "good starts and help." She told Bethenia to just up and leave him. For her father's sake Bethenia returned to her husband. But after he had lost his temper one night and whipped their sickly child for crying too much after feeding him six hard-boiled eggs at supper, Bethenia wrapped her baby in a blanket and fled for good.

So there she was, before she was eighteen, back in her father's house; in her own opinion, broken in spirit and health, bearing the dark stigma of divorce and the responsibility of a frail two-year-old child, and convinced that she would "never be happy or strong again."

But Bethenia could not be inactive long. She decided that she must have an education at all costs, and firmly pushing down her pride, she went back to school, though it meant attending classes with her younger brothers and sisters. In two months she was through the third reader, studying more advanced geography, spelling, writing, and arithmetic on the side.

All through her twenties she alternately attended school and taught school, always supporting herself and her child by any manner of work that presented itself: washing, ironing, sewing, picking berries, acting as a practical nurse.

During those hard years, when every minute counted toward her ambitions, she established a regimen that she was to adhere to throughout life: early rising, cold baths, regular exercise. She boarded around from place to place, living wherever it was cheapest. Once she took up residence with her child in the old deserted parsonage at Skipanon, which had long been unoccupied and had been used for storing hay. Proud, independent, self-willed, and apparently very charming, Bethenia refused all offers of help, even from kindly old family friends who would have given her an education on credit. This was a sort of stiff-necked and foolish pride that she deplored in later years. Five o'clock of any morning saw her at her tasks, though often two o'clock of the same night would have found her awake, rigid with cold and fatigue, in the chair in which she had been sitting at work.

So she labored and studied "by the light of a pitch stick, or a tow string in a broken mug of refuse kitchen grease." Inevitably the day came when, in the best literary tradition of the period, her remorseful husband arrived unannounced on a cold winter's night to beg her once more to return to him and to ask the privilege of seeing his child. "He found, alas for him," reported Bethenia, "not the young, ignorant, inexperienced child-mother whom he had neglected and misused, but a full-grown, self-reliant, self-supporting woman, who could look upon him only with pity."

Bethenia finally went to the flourishing little town of Roseburg and took to millinery — and this marked the beginning of her rise in the world. She went to making hats because it was one of the respectable occupations in which a woman might earn a living wage in the 1860's and '70's. Even in millinery she was no plodder. When a trained competitor opened a shop near by, Bethenia, the amateur, perceiving that she must do better or take second place locally, promptly borrowed money and went off to San Francisco to learn the trade professionally. When she came back she installed one of the first show windows in southern Oregon, and sent out invitations to a Grand Opening which launched her success and made possible the savings for her subsequent career.

For with money in her pocket and the millinery trade in all its ramifications no longer a mystery, Bethenia Owens could hardly stay interested in cutting over last year's milans. None of her customers guessed that she had taken to studying Gray's *Anatomy* in between bleaching straws, cutting over big leghorns to the currently chic pancake size, attaching bugle fringe to crowns. The only people who knew she had the book on anatomy were the doctor from whom she borrowed it and a kindly judge who saw it in her hand.

If she had expected any encouragement from friends and acquaintances when she announced at the age of thirty-two that she intended to go east to study medicine, she was due to be disappointed. Probably she did not expect encouragement. She had often burned in articulate rage, and was to burn oftener in the future, at such current commonplaces about women's place and powers as: "God shield us from the evil days that will come upon this nation when women are given the ballot, for no chain is stronger than the weakest link. So no nation can be stronger than its weakest people, who are Indians, Chinamen, idiots and women." Susan B. Anthony, on a Western tour, had come to Roseburg to lecture and had spent the night with the little milliner. All her life Bethenia was to remember walking to the hall where Miss Anthony was to speak, and hearing as they walked the raucous strains of music from the free dance hastily organized to keep the public away from such dangerous females.

One of the few women who gave Bethenia support in her ambitions was the Oregon feminist Abigail Scott Duniway, who, as we have seen, was already running her women's newspaper and knew something about the lot of independent females in the late nineteenth century. Unlike most of the other mothers among Bethenia's acquaintance, Abigail with her six children saw nothing shocking in the fact that Mrs. Owens was setting off to become a doctor the same year her grown son went to California to start his medical career.

Old Jesse Applegate, who had dandled Bethenia on his knee as a child crossing the plains to Oregon, sat down "while tending another man's sheep" to express in writing a point of view rare for men of the period. Jesse Applegate encouraged her to go east and further her career rather than settle down with some small-town suitor.

"Marriage and motherhood were not intended for you by the Creator. He designed for you a higher destiny and you will attain it."

Yet the sage of Yoncalla was no feminist. Indeed, he was always advising Bethenia against too much fervent talk about politics and woman suffrage. His formal written words on the subject come down the years with all the dignity of simple truth:

"In your own person and pursuits you give the highest proof of the equality of the human intellect, and an examplar as to the branches of human knowledge to which that of the female should be directed. In the broad and as yet unexplored fields of science there is plenty of room for all minds to act without jostling each other, and to labor in the fields of knowledge in which the dress of flesh which Nature has placed upon them is not an incumbrance."

Bethenia, however, was well along in life before she found her dress of flesh anything but an encumbrance. She once admitted that up to the age of thirty-five her great consuming regret was the fact that she had not been born a boy. "For," said she, "I realized early in life that a girl was hampered and hemmed in on all sides simply by the accident of sex."

Though Jesse Applegate might tell her that she was designed for a higher destiny than marriage and motherhood, she was by no means unattractive to men. And she so obviously enjoyed the memories of her conquests as a young "grass widow" that her book of *Life Experiences* contains no fewer than eight pages of valentines in verse sent to her in the sixties by burning swains:

THE REBEL

The very name each pulse alarms;
And oft, though vain, the wish would start,
That vine-like I'd a thousand arms
To press thee, to clasp thee, to my heart.

She is modest, but not bashful;
Free and easy, but not bold;
Like an apple, ripe and mellow,
Not too young and not too old.
Half inviting, half repulsing;
Now advancing, and now shy;
There is mischief in her dimple;
There is danger in her eye.

Judging from her memoirs, none of these ardent gentlemen
encouraged her in her vaulting ambition to become a doctor.
Indeed, her only other notable champion among men was the
Honorable Stephen Chadwick, the judge who had seen her
with Gray's *Anatomy* in her hand and guessed her secret interest long before it became public property. Judge Chadwick
spoke simple heartening words that she never forgot: "Go
ahead! You have it in you."

Local women gave her no more backing when she first announced her plans, than they were to give her months later
when she walked out of the shed on the fringes of town having
performed an autopsy on the corpse of a pauper. Indeed, before she took the stage to California en route east, they made
a point of coming to tell her without mincing words that she
was crazy; that they might buy their hats from her, but they
would certainly never consult her as a physician. No, nor any
other woman who presumed to take up a calling so obviously
designed for males.

Bethenia knew the answer to that: "The delicate and sympathetic office of a physician belongs more to my sex than to
the other, and I will enter it, and make it an honor to women."

But no one would listen. She was quite alone.

"My family felt that they were disgraced and even my own
child was influenced and encouraged to think that I was doing
him an irreparable injury by my course. People sneered and

laughed derisively. Most of my friends seemed to consider it their Christian duty to advise against, and endeavor to prevent me from taking this 'fatal' step. That crucial fortnight was a period in my life never to be forgotten. I was literally kept on the rack."

But off she went, with her head held high, in the stagecoach bound for the South and then for the East. She came back with her head still high, and she held it up after the autopsy and after she got to Portland and opened her offices as a "bath doctor" — the only rating to which at this time a woman might aspire.

She built up a flourishing practice within the set limitations of the period, and by 1878 she was ready to take a new step. Years of going to school and working to make more money in order to go to school some more had established a habit in Bethenia. She had it in mind to win a degree that would make her a bona fide physician, and she determined to force her way into the Jefferson Medical College in Philadelphia. She would, of course, be the first and only woman to be allowed to enter, but that thought did not stop her.

Away she went again to Philadelphia and straight to the head of the college to make her plea. But though this gentleman looked at her "with moist and sympathetic eyes" and spoke "in the gentlest and softest tones" and called her his "dear little woman," he could not grant the privilege. The regents would never allow it. "They would be simply shocked, scandalized and enraged at the mere mention." Why not, he suggested, go instead to the University of Michigan, where women were accepted on equal terms without having to beg and plead for an education?

Bethenia followed his advice. For nine months she worked sixteen hours a day, and in holiday time ten hours a day. In two years she had her degree — two hard years without a day of illness, thanks, she was sure, to her strict regimen of rising at four, taking a cold shower and vigorous exercise, allowing one half hour for each meal, retiring every night at ten. From the University of Michigan she went to Chicago for clinical work and then back to the university for post-graduate work, in which her son now joined her. After this she felt she needed a reward, and with a bag full of letters bearing the impressive, if unrecognizable, seal of the state of Oregon she sailed for Europe to visit hospitals, watch famous surgeons operate, and "see the sights."

When Bethenia returned to Portland the days of being a bath doctor, charging one dollar and a half for electric and medicated baths, were definitely behind her. She began then to enjoy real local fame. Former enemies and decriers became friends and well-wishers. Even the one-time rival milliner of Roseburg presented herself as a pale and trembling patient and gave Bethenia the opportunity to clasp her hand and thank her for putting obstacles in her path and forcing her out of the easy complacency of a second-rate success in hat-making.

"You see," Bethenia explained to the bewildered woman, "a friend once said to me, 'If I wished to increase your height two and a half inches I would attempt to press you down, and you would grow upward from sheer resentment.' "

Bethenia's later life gave her many chances to savor the bitter-sweet experience of seeing one-time detractors become admirers attempting to curry favor. And she was human enough to notice and record these instances. One event in particular occupies some pages of her memoirs:

Back in the days when she took whatever work she could find to support herself and her child she had done three weeks of hard labor for a prosperous farmer's family; labor which consisted in taking care of a sick mother and a newborn infant, her own four-year-old boy and two other children, cooking for eleven people — including four hired men — caring for the milk from ten cows, doing all the washing and ironing, feeding the chickens, carrying all the wood she needed up a flight of stairs. When it came time to collect her fee she timidly asked five dollars a week. The surly farmer, who had expected to pay three, said she would have to take it out in an order on a store. Here she was obliged to accept inferior goods at a high price. Bethenia knew that the farmer paid his hired men two dollars

a day besides giving them room and board and Sundays off.
She told herself in bitterness that some day she would "show"
this man. And fate allowed her to. At the height of her career
as a public figure in Oregon she was on a railroad train bound
for the state capitol, surrounded by prominent men all seeking
a word with her. The farmer who had treated her so badly came
pushing through the crowd anxious to show that he knew her.

"She received him politely," Dr. Owens wrote of herself in
the third person, "but . . . she could not find it in her heart to
be cordial, and he soon retired, discomfited."

With the passing of the years Bethenia spoke out in public
more rather than less, in spite of the warnings of old Mr.
Applegate. The subjects on which she felt qualified to hold
a positive opinion had a wide range. She publicly decried the
church's hypocritical attitude toward illegitimate children.
She fervently encouraged the well-born young ladies of Portland to defy the ban on skating as a rough sport. She wrote
letters to the press taking issue with President Eliot of Har-
vard, who, she asserted, thought that "post-graduate studies
were conducive to celibacy." Eliot criticized women for their
growing wish to develop their muscular system and increase
their physical strength. Dr. Owens was pleased to remind him
that the physical burdens of women were more arduous than
those of men and that anything which stimulated circulation
and muscle tone was all to the good.

She took lengthy issue with a certain Mr. Tallack who had
injudiciously expressed in public his growing alarm at the disuse of the side-saddle. Tallack claimed that women because
of their anatomical structure rode more comfortably at a sixty-
or seventy-degree angle.

"Oh, no, Mr. Tallack," replied Bethenia in the newspapers.
"God gave women legs for their use, and for the same use to
which he gave them to men. . . . He [Tallack] says men's legs
are long and flat and women's are short and round. Well, in
my time I have seen a good many women with long legs and a
good many men with short ones. It was often said of Senator
Douglas that he was taller sitting down than he was standing

up . . ." and so on, until the unfortunate Mr. Tallack must have regretted the fact that a woman with an understanding of anatomy had seen fit to contradict him.

Side-saddles, in Bethenia's opinion, would soon belong only in museums. Furthermore, she prophesied that in the not far-distant future people would look back and laugh at the tempest that was stirred up over the appearance of "ladies" in the streets without their hats. On the grounds of health, Bethenia supported the novel custom of occasionally emerging without a hat. Hair was not harmed by sun and fresh air, she declared. She recalled the day when, driving wildly through the streets of Portland with a frantic husband to the home where his wife, as he supposed, lay "dying," she had been summoned in her carriage to the curb by the agitated signaling of two women friends.

When she drew up, they came around to her side of the buggy and whispered in shocked dismay: "Bethenia, do you know you are hatless?"

As a matter of fact, Bethenia didn't. She had left in too great a hurry. "Why didn't you tell me I didn't have my hat?" she cried in horror to the desperate husband, and then, seeing the expression on his face and realizing the absurdity of the situation, she burst into laughter and laughed all the way to the house where her patient lay. The next day with equanimity she looked in the newspapers for the caricature of herself that she fully expected to find. None appeared. Presumably the disgraceful story had not been circulated.

In 1884 Bethenia fell in love and took time out to make a romantic marriage. She was forty-four when she married Colonel John Adair and hyphenated her name as Owens-Adair. At the age of forty-seven she gave birth to her second child, a daughter. Bethenia felt her life to be completely fulfilled. Her career had flowered beyond her dreams, she had made a happy marriage, she had given birth to a daughter, for whom she planned a professional life like her own. For three days she lay in her bed and made pictures of the opportunities she would place in her daughter's lap. In her formative years she would interest her in medicine by taking her on calls. She would make available to her all the libraries and special schools into which women were slowly beginning to push their dogged way. In her daughter she would see realized every hope of her own life. . . . And then the child died.

For the first time in forty-seven years Bethenia's spirit broke. Ill and despondent, she was finally unable to carry on her practice. She moved with her husband to a remote farm near Astoria, and here she returned to the pioneer hardships of her early youth. Here also in time she returned to the practice of medicine. For she could not refuse to help the isolated hard-driven people who were her "neighbors" within a radius of twenty miles.

Night after night a lantern would flash across her window in the farmhouse and she would rise in the darkness, dress hastily, and go out to listen to the hushed and tense story of some frightened farmer. She would put on her high boots and her heavy coat and set out with him. Sometimes she went on horseback, sometimes on foot, pressing her way through sharp wire grass, wading in swamps, cutting fallen trees to make a path. Sometimes she went by boat, sitting huddled in the bow as the man rowed against a howling wind.

Before many years this hard life made inroads on Bethenia's robust constitution. She was forced to change climates, and she went north to the high dry inland country of Yakima in the state of Washington, where her career had another blooming.

During the Yakima period Bethenia thought nothing of driving twenty or thirty miles by day or night in making visits. As a typical story of this period she has left an account of her activities during sixty hours of a diphtheria epidemic.

The disease first struck the widely removed branches of a country family and kept her driving for days without rest, from house to house in bitter snowy weather. This family's ordeal culminated finally in a scene in one of the farmhouses where the shock of the death of the beloved and beautiful young daughter brought on in the son's wife the pangs of premature labor and sent the mother temporarily out of her mind with grief. Bethenia, beset and exhausted, managed finally to get the nearest health officer on the telephone. She told him that he must come at once to remove the contamination of the corpse from a house in which a baby was about to be born. The health officer replied that he was engaged in a special Elks celebration, but would try to make it in the morning with the undertaker. Bethenia did not report her further conversation, but she did report that both men arrived that same night.

Afterwards she could not help boasting a little — again in the third person:

"Thus, during sixty consecutive hours, Dr. Adair, then in her sixty-fifth year, accomplished an almost incredible amount of labor, under great mental strain (as the parties were her warm personal friends as well as patients) having traveled in that time over one hundred miles, with but two hours sleep out of the whole sixty hours, and without extreme exhaustion — a record very few male physicians, if any could equal, and surely none could excel."

When she finally left Yakima and active practice, she drove alone with her favorite horse down the Columbia River. It was late autumn and all her friends and acquaintances advised against it, fearing she might be caught in early snow. But Bethenia defied them as usual and liked later to recall this peaceful, leisurely journey back to Portland, during which she visited former acquaintances and even collected an old bill or two.

Although she went to California to write her memoirs, she did not sit down in the sun to wait for death. Bethenia lived to be well past eighty, and the last twenty years of her life were the most significant of all. By the force of her knowledge, her energy, and her determination she managed to bring to passage in the state of Oregon bills to sterilize the insane and to require medical examinations for all people seeking a marriage license.

She led up to her great campaign by using the columns of newspapers and by making public speeches on the subject of mental health and the necessity for eugenic improvement.

Over and over again she would tell the story of how the determination to fight the perpetuation of insanity came to her.

She was being conducted through the Oregon State Insane Asylum and, sickened by the spectacle of mental degeneracy, she said to the officiating doctor:

" 'This is a horrible phase of life. When is it to end?'

" 'I don't know,' he replied.

" 'If I had the power,' I continued, 'I would curtail it, for I would see to it that not one of this class should ever be permitted to curse the world with offspring.'

"He said, 'Would you advocate that method?'

" 'I would certainly, if I were not a woman, and a woman M.D., to whom I know too well at this day and age, it would simply mean ostracism.' "

When, twenty years after this episode, Dr. Owens-Adair no longer feared ostracism, she began her long, grim fight. She was determined to have all the mentally unfit rendered incapable of producing their kind. To this end she wanted a law passed to sterilize those found insane, and to require any mentally unsound human being to be rendered sterile before being permitted to marry.

When in 1907 she first presented her bill in Oregon, it was dismissed as "unfit for public discussion." She then tried it in the state of Washington, where a brave Senator introduced it. It was greeted with "coarse laughter and coarser jest."

By 1909 she was back with the bill again in Oregon. This time the Senate received it kindly and passed it over to the House with a two-thirds vote. "The House greeted it with smiles and passed it on to the Governor with his little axe."

Undaunted by the veto, Bethenia had the bill ready again in 1911. Again it failed. "Two more years of waiting, worry, and expense."

In 1913 the bill was reintroduced and passed, but was handed over to the people of Oregon who, after a vigorous campaign by powerful church forces, voted it down.

In 1917 she had the bill revised to create a State Board of Eugenics, composed of the State Board of Health and the heads of various state institutions having insane, criminal, or feeble-minded persons in their charge. Men and women were to be sterilized only on decision of this board, and subjects were to have the right to appeal to a circuit court.

This last bill passed, the expected referendum against it failed to materialize, and it became law, only to be declared unconstitutional in the famous case of Cline vs. The State Board of Eugenics. This was a case involving a sixty-six-year-old man who had criminally attacked a small girl and who was ordered to be sterilized by the State Board of Eugenics. A Portland lawyer saw his chance of notoriety and took up Cline's case. Through a technicality the case was turned down in circuit court, and since there was no means provided for carrying it to the Supreme Court the whole question was again stalemated.

Dr. Bethenia's only comment was: "So after fifteen years of fighting we must begin all over again!"

This new fight was not a long one. In February 1922 Governor West signed H. B. 69, the Lewelling Sterilization Bill, and the Portland *Journal* could write: "The successful outcome of the bill is considered a personal triumph for Dr. Owens-Adair." In the same year she brought out a book so bold that it had to be published privately: *Human Sterilization — Its Social and Legislative Aspects.*

Bethenia never tapered off. She finally just quit. Had she exercised her own choice in the matter, it seems likely that she might have asked to have carved on her tombstone the caustic words of a former neighbor from the Clatsop Plains. Contrasting the harum-scarum Bethenia with her sister, who was a "perfect lady," he remarked that Bethenia "thought she could do anything a boy could, and was just as good and maybe a little better."

X. Dear Diary

1

PIONEER WOMEN of the Far West, by the records they left for posterity, rendered a service to some possible future anthropologist who will be able to study American females of the nineteenth and early twentieth centuries with the cool detachment with which today the natives of Peru or the Navajos of New Mexico are observed. Not only did the wilderness diarists, letter-writers, and autobiographers of the years between 1830 and 1900 leave material by which the reaction of women to a primitive environment might be learned; they also made possible the tracing of less obvious aspects of feminine nature. Within fixed boundaries of space and time, set forth boldly against an uncluttered background, we can see emerging the hidden drives of the American woman. Beginning with the soul-searchings of Narcissa Whitman and Mary Walker, following with the first women's club, the Columbia Maternal Association, and ending with Abigail Scott Duniway signing the Suffrage Proclamation, or Dr. Bethenia Owens-Adair winning her fight for the sterilization of the insane, it is possible to trace the evolution from personal to social awareness in the American female.

The strongest feeling that comes over the researcher who digs into the pages — both dull and rewarding — of diaries, journals, letters, and reminiscences of the pioneer period is one of gratitude for those who found the time and energy to leave a record of any kind behind them. It is a curious urge that prompts people to take notes on their daily lives as they live them. Perhaps it springs wholly from the ego, and perhaps it is a gift of foresight. Whatever it is, most people lack it. They reflect the attitude of the grandmother who wrote: "I have to cry now as I recall those old days. I didn't know those common every-day things would be history."

This, Rebecca West would say, is woman displaying her chief

defect, that of idiocy — finding the meaning of the word in the Greek root of "idiot," signifying "private person." Intent on their private lives, says Miss West, most women are as unaware of the significance of great events about them as an idiot would be. She develops the theme far enough, you may remember, to accuse men at the same time of lunacy, or the tendency to see the world as by moonlight, which shows the outlines of every object without revealing the details by which its true nature may be known.

It is just by virtue of the private quality of their lives and their necessary preoccupation with details that we have reason to be so thankful to those pioneer women who detached themselves enough from the daily round to make comment on it — though that comment extend no farther than a humdrum notation in an intermittent journal. "O dear! How can I tell it. Squash again for breakfast." "John rattles like dry peapods now that he got his deerskin suit soaked on Wednesday." "Today . . . took hold of horse flesh with pretty good relish." "This winter finds me fully occupied as ever & what I write must be done in a hurry amidst all the noise & confusion of a kitchen filled with children & Indians besides a German agent who is spending a few weeks with us . . . a professed Botanist."

By such comment, from simple women whose lives were bounded by the clearings in which their cabins stood, we are able to piece together pictures of the period of the last frontier, so near us in point of time though already so far removed in experience. Undeniably any intelligent woman can tell us more about what life was actually like in the Far West in early days than we could ever get from the reports of a dozen explorers intent on the main theme of conquest of a strange land by force.

2

First of all, life in the wilderness challenged every woman to become her essentially ingenious and resourceful self, that inventive and persistent creature who made civilization in the domestic sense possible. Of necessity each pioneer performed woman's immemorial role of provider and civilizer. But not only did she learn to search the now neglected book of Nature for foods, medications, and clues to the weather; she set about the taming of the wild countryside as soon as she put foot in it. Around the edges of the flower garden she had insisted on tearing by main force from the coastal wilderness, she placed borders of clamshells or bleached sea biscuits, with their delicately incised pattern. Inland she confined her precious wallflowers and peonies within rows of empty whisky bottles or lumps of the weird and whimsical minerals that abound in dry Western country. Where old missions of the French Fathers had ruined into decay she found and rescued a "mission rose." She cultivated a puny pink until it was carnation size and could win prizes for her daughter at a later county fair. "This too is important," silently said the slips from the sweetbrier — brought all the way from Illinois — that she passed out seasonally to other women lacking vines for their cabin porches.

Since the pioneer woman lived close to the seasons, whose changes were of such vital moment in her domestic economy, she was keenly aware of time. Awareness of time made her a keeper of records. The first vital statistics in old Oregon are to be found in the minute-book of the Columbia Maternal Association: the lists of the members, the dates on which they joined, the dates of their children's births and deaths. Washington State College has a faded letter to Elkanah Walker from the Hudson's Bay factor at Fort Colville begging the birth dates of the factor's half-Indian sons who were being sent off to Europe for their education. The factor remembered, he wrote, that Mrs. Walker jotted down these dates in her "pocket Book" when she visited them. Like many another early woman Mary was playing, quite unconsciously, the role of a genealogist.

Hardly were the feet of the pioneer woman off a dirt floor and on a wooden one, hardly had her men cut the first trail through the forest or sunk the first well by the river, before she was trying to find a common ground on which to meet with other women. As far back as 1840 the missionary wives were turning in their minds and on their tongues such pressing problems as how to enlist the "aid and cooperation" of their husbands in training their children; how to prevent the shameless Indians from exerting on "minds and morals" a deleterious non-Puritan influence.

Into their diaries and their letters went subjective questionings. The heaviest household tasks did not keep these women from a concern with their own motivations, their actions, and their personal destiny. Far oftener than one might think, they recognized the split between what life demanded of them and what potentially they might have been. The seeds of discontent were fermenting in secret many years before they came into the open.

3

If, however, we look at this generic woman of the nineteenth century less with the eye of an anthropologist, we should begin with her administering creature comforts.

In the early days women were the only doctors. Under necessity they evolved out of their meager store of supplies, and from nature, certain simple remedies in which they had confidence. They checked bleeding with cobwebs, or with wheat flour — when they had it — and salt in a poultice. Wet earth was applied to bites and stings, as were also scrapings from fresh vegetables, and bread and milk poultices. Sunflower seeds soaked in a pint of spirits, allowed to stand for twelve hours and taken internally, were considered a sure cure for rheumatism. Whisky played a vital role in home medicine and was freely prescribed for everything from inflammatory rheumatism to snakebite. Salt pork chopped up with onions served for attacks of what we would call tonsillitis today. Onion syrup was a remedy beloved of children for the inevitable winter cold.

When a neighbor became sick the nearest woman went to her aid, often walking many miles, sometimes knitting stockings as she walked — though these must surely have been the women who were without fear of Indian or animal, or without curiosity or interest in the life of the forest.

"People say to me," wrote an old lady at the turn of the century, " 'What did you do for a doctor?' We worked hard, ate hearty and slept sound. When we felt indisposed we took a tea made of wild cherry and dogwood bark and rested a while. The first doctor that came to the country was Dr. Casto. Then the people began to get sick and they have wanted a doctor ever since."

Not all ailments yielded so readily to wild cherry and dogwood bark and a short rest. Women with serious internal disorders, often incident to ignorant care at the time of childbirth, had to die with no relief for their pain. Diaries like that of Mrs. Ebey of Whidby Island create a picture of a woman in the grip of an intolerable physical agony, which, indeed, carried her off at the age of thirty:

"I am getting well again perhaps only for a short period — health and life uncertain. Although this is a healthy climate my constitution appears to be very much injured. . . . I grieved a great deal in the night when all was sound asleep. . . . I am alone and no person who can take interest in my welfare to converse with and thus I have a great deal of time to think. I pray the Lord to uphold me and enable me to bear it with more patience lest I wear my body down and become unable to raise my family."

4

Next to medical aid in a still undeveloped country, food was the most vital of all the problems. Knowledge of calories was not yet available, but any woman knew her children could not thrive on a straight diet of squash and berries, or salmon and boiled potatoes, or bread made of a "wheat" that consisted of cooked and mashed potatoes mixed with a little grain, parched in a skillet and ground in a coffee mill. Some pioneer women availed themselves of Indian knowledge, took lessons in making bread from the camas root, in getting flour from the seeds of the great white water lilies that floated on the Klamath marshes in Oregon, from the brake fern, or from the wappato roots that naked squaws deftly gathered with their toes in the sloughs of the Columbia River.

A few whites learned to cook and eat the bulb of the seashore flag, which resembled the Jerusalem artichoke, and to dig for the edible sunflower roots. Many more dried the seasonal berry crops, the wild plums and grapes. Sweets were rare. There was no sugar, not even honey, for domestic bees had to be brought all the way overland from the East. Milk was a luxury. A woman who could not nurse her newborn child was in a desperate plight. On the coast there were clams, and clam juice often helped children through the weaning period and invalids to regain strength. But clams can become in time a very monotonous diet, as the wit from the state of Washington implied in Congress when he remarked that during hard times the settlers of the Pacific Northwest had subsisted so exclusively on clams that "their stomachs rose and fell with the tides."

A valuable record was made of early life on Fourth Plain, not far from Vancouver, Washington, in which we can see in detail women playing their part in the simple rural existence of pioneer days.

Farming, said Elizabeth Gedney, who wrote it, was done mainly by proverb:

> Clay on sand, makes good land
> But sand on clay, is thrown away.

or:

> Sow in the sop,
> 'Twill be heavy atop.

Both men and women could read the coming weather by signs in the world of nature. A certain mountain was watched every spring for melting snow. When the peak of Silver Star showed naked, they knew the frosts would not reappear. Lacking a mountain, these amateur prophets advised waiting until the hazelnuts were the size of a squirrel's ear. Then it was safe to put in seeds. In the spring if the ash tree leafed out before the oak, there would be a dry summer. If the oak showed green first, they prepared for a wet season.

They knew there would not be rain on a day when the morning grass held canopies of spiders' webs — for these sensible creatures would hardly spend a night on such extensive and intricate handiwork just for the elements to destroy. The gentle fuzzy black and orange caterpillars that abounded in late summer acted as a living code to be deciphered by sharp eyes. "If the head end was longer than the tail, one might be confident that rain was due. If the tail was longer, it would be safe to delay harvesting."

The moon, too, gave signs. When it appeared in such a position that if it were full of water it would certainly be spilling over, then they got in the crops at once. If, however, it rode the sky like a boat, the hay was safe. These were the "wet and dry" moons, known also to Indians.

The moon guided them also in planting. When it was waxing they put into the earth those vegetables that grew above ground: peas, beans, squash. When it was on the wane they planted root vegetables: carrots, potatoes, turnips, all tubers. "The theory was that as the moon ascended the plants ascended, and as the moon went down anything newly planted would go down too." Good Friday was the day of days for planting.

5

Women were forever experimenting with the limitations of their diet, to keep children and menfolk from complaining or from developing a driving hunger for sweets that nothing could satisfy. They made salads of the green shoots of wild gooseberry, pies of sorrel and salal, jams of Oregon grape, wild currant and plum. They preserved blackberries by thrusting them one at a time into small-necked bottles. They fried doughnuts in bear's grease when there was no shortening, used deer's rennet for cheese-making when there was no calf's rennet, stuffed bear cub for Thanksgiving dinner when there was no pig. They stripped the leafy stalks of dry-land sunflower to eat like celery, made "sugar," in the corn and melon country of the interior, from watermelon centers strained and added to the juice of boiled corncobs.

Salt pork was their most essential staple. For butter for "Sunday cake" they melted it down and strained it through a bit of muslin. They could stretch a stewing hen by cooking the pork with it, as the pork took on the chicken flavor. Cracklings from the pork were also cooked with dog or "calico" salmon (inferior to the Chinook) in a big pot with boiled potatoes. Pork went into the baked-bean pot too, layer after layer of it, along with molasses, over the beans that had been soaked Friday and boiled on Saturday "until when you took some in a spoon and blew on them the shells would split." The rest of Saturday and up to noon Sunday they baked in a slow oven for the immemorial Sunday stand-by.

Wild birds with too gamy a taste were tamed for the table by experimental cookings. A cut onion in the pan with wood duck, for instance, supposedly took up its too wild flavor. Tomatoes, which were not eaten raw as they were said to be poisonous in that state, were used in a variety of ways: when ripe, their boiled-down juice sweetened with honey was served on hotcakes; green they were stewed, sieved, stewed again with salt, pepper, and cloves to make a flavoring for stews and gravies; or they appeared in mincemeat in place of meat or apples. Wrote Mary Walker of her first Thanksgiving in old Oregon: "Succeeded very tolerably in making mince pies without apples."

Descriptions survive of meals with a last-century amplitude and succulence. The women of the colony of Christian Communists at Aurora, Oregon, were famed for their cookery. Travelers in late pioneer days came from far and wide to feast on their chicken cooked in garlic, their venison and smoked hams, their extra-deep deep-dish apple pie.

The matter of food has remained of utmost importance on the frontier down to the present, for men who live exclusively on bacon, bread, beans, and coffee readily develop scurvy. In the inland country and in mining camps, right up to modern times, green vegetables had to be carted in from distant Utah and California, and were never as important cargo for the heavily loaded freight wagons as whisky. But even without womenfolk to advise them, miners and backwoodsmen in the Far West finally learned to carry sacks of potatoes twenty miles through deep snow to keep themselves from this dreaded disease. Uncooked potatoes, sliced up and soaked in vinegar, were considered the "sovereign" remedy.

On the whole their boring diet was certainly one of the factors that intensified men's wish for a woman to struggle with cooking at the open fire or on the ramshackle wood-burning stove in cabin or shanty. There are still plenty of men in the Far West who couldn't read a menu in a restaurant with any ease; men like old Mose from Idaho's Banner Mine who threw the bill of fare angrily on the floor and roared: "Don't try to cram any book larnin' down me. Grub's what I want! Grub — and damn quick too!"

One must put in for the record, however, that it was men, not women, who developed the famous sour-dough biscuit of the range and cattle country, unstintedly praised by those who made and ate it. From a cattleman who could whip up in no time a respectable meal of beans, and potatoes, with apples and onions fried together, and fresh-caught fish cooked with bacon comes an exact description of the sour-dough process:

"The modern baker hasn't gained much when he don't know the secret of sourdough. When you get the fresh milk in the morning you fill your sourdough pot, add flour, and thoroughly work it till you get a good thick batter. Then you set it behind the stove where it will keep warm for five or six hours . . . let it raise and sour. When you are ready to make your biscuit, you add salt and soda and some fresh flour, pinch off your big fat biscuits, roll them in melted lard, and let them set fifteen or twenty minutes to make their chemical change, then put them in a hot oven to bake. There's no other biscuit worth bothering about when you've been used to sourdough."

6

Not every woman who got west was a domestic paragon. Some shiftless, lowborn, and disreputable females — by no means smart enough for parlor houses — reached the Far West, though descendants of pioneers would like you to believe that all such riffraff dropped beside the way in some name-less state on the wrong side of the Rockies.

Consider the woman of Texas Jack. Texas Jack was a "cattle killer and a horse thief" who lived up one of the many Rattle-snake Canyons in desert country. Who his woman was or "how she got that way we neither learned nor cared," recalls her terse chronicler. "It was in the winter. The woman's hands were covered with stockings instead of mittens." Though it was in late pioneer days, "Texas Jack's woman had never seen a carpet on the floor. She thought carpets were made to be rolled up and stood in a corner. A distant aunt of hers had a carpet once, she said, but it stood in a corner."

One single authority only need be cited to indicate that women who could not keep a house clean or make respectable pie crust were to be found. Thomas Donaldson, in *Idaho of Yesterday*, devotes some pages to a spirited criticism of the stage stations that lay along the rough highways in the period immediately following the prairie schooner. These stations — about fifty or sixty miles apart, a day's run — provided shelter for horses and travelers and were, in truth, miniature forts from which frequent attacks of the Indians were withstood.

These one-story log houses, complained Mr. Donaldson bit-terly, were "rich in little but dirt." Food consisted of bacon and "white-lead" bread. There was never chicken to be had, although Mr. Donaldson remembered being compelled to drive away scores of them in order to pass through the door. The pies consisted of a "sole-leather lard-soaked lower crust, half-baked, with a thin veneer of fried apples daubed with brown sugar." A large pot of mustard invariably graced the center of the table. In it rested an iron spoon which had succumbed in part to the attack of the vinegar. This mustard traveled freely around the table to lend the jaded victuals a false air of piquancy. Although there were plenty of cows at that time, the calves, not the travelers, got the milk, because, it is sug-gested, their owners found it too much trouble to milk.

On the whole, however, shiftless females were the exception. Western existence did not permit many women the luxury of being lazy. The life demanded of them a standard of conduct that fell little short of heroism. Yet though it was difficult in the Far West to avoid acting the part of a heroine, women did not think of themselves in such a role. They quietly accepted as a part of the pioneer experience the necessity for courage and endurance in the face of any emergency.

Far too many individual pioneer women have been forgotten. Self-effacing wives and mothers remain nameless where posthumous fame is the reward of those who by virtue of their eccentricity or their degradation early made a place for themselves in pioneer memories and in the index of many a Western book. It is far easier to remember names like Mother Damnable or the Little Gold Dollar than it is prosaic Mary Jones or Lucy Smith.

The stories of many hard-working, cheerful, indomitable females were too ordinary (by the standards of the times) to make a lasting impression. But from library files, museum shelves, and yarns of old-timers come tantalizing fragments, scraps of plot, hints of personalities that tease and haunt the inquiring mind.

One would like to know more of Mrs. David Blaine, the spicy-tongued wife of Seattle's first minister. During the Indian uprising she was rowed out to the gunboat *Decatur* and carried aboard in an armchair with her newborn infant. Calmly and with humor she wrote home of her life in the first weeks after childbirth — going back and forth on a stormy sea in a small boat to tend to her domestic duties in an abandoned log cabin, although hostile Indians might be lurking behind any shrub or tree.

"The babe," she wrote, "is a month old today and I guess has been tossed about as much as a child of his age ever was. The ship is some distance from shore so that we have to go back and forth in a small boat. He has been taken ashore some half dozen times or more. I have been off to wash and iron and do some other work. He stands it pretty well though he cries considerably from wind on his stomach, is as fat as a pig and dreadfully homely."

Then there was a Catherine Maynard, also of Seattle, whose midnight ride to "save Seattle" during this same period is a subject for debate among old-timers, some of whom gravely question that it ever took place. But it is too good a story to be omitted from Western lore, with Mrs. Maynard setting out in the dead of a stormy night to paddle fourteen miles across the bay to warn the east-side settlers that the Indians were arming and to let the *Decatur* know of the danger. The canoe was guided by Sally, a daughter of Chief Kitsap — equal in importance, though not so well known to history as the other friendly chief, Seattle. Five Indian women and a man, so legend has it, went along to keep the frail craft riding the wild waves. When they were blown up on the shore at one point where hostile Indians were waiting, the quick-witted red women told them that the bulky form in the bottom of the boat was only a sack of clams. It was really Catherine Maynard. They made the trip to the *Decatur* and back before daylight, so that their journey would not be known to other suspicious Indians.

Whether Mrs. Maynard "saved" Seattle or not may be a subject of debate. It is not debatable, however, that she did plant the first wild dandelions for use in medications. Her husband, "Doc" Maynard, was a Seattle character of the rough-and-ready type, who practiced medicine and established the first crude hospital. The dark forests spreading to the very edge of the tidewaters provided no natural home for the golden-faced bloom. Mrs. Maynard was a practical nurse, and owing to her wish for the medicinal aid of the dandelion this stubborn and hardy plant now gives Northwest gardeners as much trouble as it does lawn-tenders in any other part of America.

Those fearless women who chastised miscreant Indians regardless of possible consequences have already been spoken of. There was Lydia Low, of Washington Territory, who caught a half-naked Indian in the act of stealing a ham from the rafters of her kitchen. She was stirring a large kettle of cornmeal mush when she saw him, and without a moment's hesitation she snatched the large wooden spoon from the hot yellow meal and applied it with direction and vigor to the Indian's bare behind. He did not linger and he left the ham.

Another woman dispersed single-handed a band of thieving Indians unable to resist the gleam of bright cooking utensils and the color of quilts hung out to air at an immigrant camp. This woman came of fighting stock, and she proceeded to wrench a tent pole out of the earth and lay about her without delay or discrimination. The next day a chief turned up to apologize for the misconduct of his men. Pointing at the heroine of the affray, he signified his unbounded admiration by offering five hundred dollars' spot cash for her.

From the compressed pages of pioneer reminiscences, heroines of less dramatic but equally stern mold emerge. There were many women left as widows, or with invalided husbands, to bring up a family and somehow earn a living in untamed country. Family tragedies are often set forth in these pages with a stark simplicity far more moving than embroidered phrasing could ever make them:

"We worked eight years on the ranch and in clearing the land we found later that we had burned away timber valued at $2,000 — and all we got out of the farm was $1,100."

Names without faces and faces without names flash on and off the crowded screen of pioneer recollections; memories briefly lit by the sparse phrasing of some old-timer whose mind has held a fading picture down the long years.

"One day early in July a widow drove up in a covered wagon with a wore-out team and two little boys and a girl. They had traveled to the end of their finances and now they wanted to sell their canary bird to raise some money. Billy bought the bird, and I took the family home with me for haying, as I needed a cook and could use the little boy. They proved to be good people but they were city trained and the country was too hard for them. They got discouraged and left."

8

No fiction could possibly excel in dramatic values the romance that presents itself, sheared of all overlay, in the recollection of simple Western people:

"My father was Frederick William Perkins. He was born in the city of New York in 1826. His father had seven trading ships as merchantmen on the ocean and owned a quarter of a mile of wharfage along New York's waterfront. His nephew became the partner of one of New York's greatest financiers. My father's mother was a Griswold.

"I mention these things because when my father married my mother, an Indian girl, descendant of chiefs, his mother cut him off with one dollar and never claimed him again as her son.

"My mother was banished from her tribe as punishment for marrying a white man.

". . . My grandfather Ske-owt-kin was a trapper for the Hudson's Bay Company and brought his furs to Angus McDonald. Ske-owt-kin means 'Shadow top' or tall man. My grandfather was tall and very strong. He could kill a deer by taking it in his hands and breaking its neck.

"My grandmother lived with us, clinging always to Indian customs. She preferred food cooked in baskets by placing hot stones among the food. I can see her yet, lifting the hot stones with two sticks and dropping them into the baskets. . . . My grandmother was my best teacher. It was she who taught me the mysteries of creation . . . besides the religion handed down from one generation to another by word of mouth. The stars, the mountains, the trees and rocks all had a meaning. . . . We might prevail upon her to sleep in the house during winter, but as soon as spring came we would miss her. We always knew then that she had set up her teepee not far away and would remain there until winter snows drove her in. . . .

". . . [Father] was the dentist and doctor for the valley. He was elected justice of the peace. They called him 'judge.'

"My earliest recollections are of teepees all around our house. In these were my father's patients. It would be called a sanitorium today. He treated these sick people and fed them right. We were poor with the rest of them but I know my father got a lot out of life that people never dreamed of."

9

There was in pioneer life not only many a hardship but also an intimacy and a robustness well remembered by those who lived on the last fringes of it.

"I taught the first school until a regular teacher could be found. I rode horseback and carried my baby on the saddle in front of me. I remember this period as the happiest time of my life."

"Mother brought the first kerosene lamp to Whidby Island. She lived the coziest and happiest years, she said, in the old three-roomed cabin with the big willows in front and the fine view from the little windows."

A pioneer of Stevens County, Washington, recalls holiday times when they "had parties and danced from Christmas until one week after the New Year." Food around the factor's house at Fort Coville was abundant: game, fish, chicken, roast pigs, puddings, and cakes. "Mother didn't do much work at that time. She would get an Indian woman to stay with the children in our cabin and she would go with the others to the factor's house for the parties. They would feast and dance all night and go home to sleep and be back the next night."

When there was a dance anywhere in the Western country, people walked or rode miles to attend it. If they had children they brought the children. Makeshift beds were put up in an attic or a loft and the children bedded down together. At midnight, when there was a supper of beans, meat, pickles, and cake, the children got up and tumbled downstairs to share it. They went back to bed then until morning, when they tumbled out again for hotcakes and whatever else the larder afforded. All night long their parents were dancing to someone's fiddling and such old swinging phrases as "Bird hop out and the Babboon in, three hands round and you go agin."

There was astounding vigor in these people — a vigor which we cannot understand today and which seems almost to have come out of the new land itself, with its untapped sources of vital energy.

10

When we move along from woman the creature of simple domestic habits, of uncomplicated pleasures and automatic responses, to woman the seeker and agitator, certain larger implications begin to show themselves.

The connecting threads between the Pacific Northwest and New England exerted an influence on pioneer Western life that cannot be denied. The majority of early Oregon pioneers who came to settle down, farm, and raise a family were of the old American stock. They left communities which were direct inheritors of New England traditions, with the difference, however, that, no longer being New England, Puritan rigidity had been somewhat slackened.

History seems to bear out the theory that there are certain geographical hot spots where life mysteriously flares up in greater intensity than in other sections of the country. This theory comes to mind when you see how alike in many respects were communities of the early Northwest and New England villages. The traditional American government by contract: "We the people . . ."; the plans for churches, libraries, and schools before there were roads; the debating societies: "This winter we organized a debating society. Decided to meet at our house because we are the only ones with a lumber floor"; all these ways of life are typically Old Oregon. They are also typically New England.

Both New England and the Far West put emphasis on education. Certain favored young women of pioneer families who had prospered early were, indeed, given the benefits of a private education before their home communities had attained the dignity of sidewalks or street lights. Young ladies in Walla Walla enjoyed a selective curriculum at St. Paul's School for Girls when their parents were still paying tuition in gold dust, six mule teams of flour, or cattle selected by the headmaster himself on the open range. Before the stumps were out of the main streets, Portland had its sedate St. Helen's Hall to educate its young ladies, and the pupils of Annie Wright's Seminary in

Tacoma, though they had to walk to chapel on two rough planks laid on a sea of mud, and light their way at night with kerosene lanterns, were enjoying the benefits of higher learning along with such *Extras — Optional* — as instruction in painting on china, plush, and velvet.

The first women in the West, as we have seen, carried with them the seeds of discontent, the faint stirrings of a new life for females, that were beginning to be apparent in parts of New England and in particular in western New York State in the late thirties and forties. The missionary wives of old Oregon reflected this new and still almost unconscious feminism in such small but significant matters as praying aloud in public — the verdict against which so agitated Narcissa Whitman. And there is a direct line of association between Lucy Larcom and the Labor Reform Association founded in Lowell in 1845 (which managed to get a ten-hour day for women passed in three states before the Civil War) and Abigail Scott Duniway's agitations in Oregon, much later in the century, for decent wages for women workers. The great national feminists were of New England extraction. They started the battle for equal suffrage, but the states of the Far West were the first to win it.

The budding feminism that was brought to the Pacific Northwest by certain outstanding pioneers had a chance to flourish in rude Western settlements where daily life offered so many novelties that women out of their accustomed "place" were not apt to occasion much comment. By the time these communities had crystallized into approximations of the old patterns, women had tested their strength and had some notion of how far it might carry them. They had proved themselves able to conquer a primitive land with a resourcefulness and a courage equal to any man's. What was there, then, that could ever stop woman? asked the more thoughtful daughters and granddaughters of sunbonnet heroines. As women they believed that the world — a new and better world — was theirs for the making. It lay, they felt certain, just around the corner.

XI. Over the Top of the World

BUT WHAT was around the corner?

In closing a chronicle of such average yet remarkable women as the Western pioneers one comes inevitably to the question: What has happened to the American woman that makes it possible for angry writers to attack her today as a creature who is lazy, parasitic, dissatisfied, and neurotic?

What has become of the symbolic little woman "no bigger 'n a pint of cider" who could carry a child over the Blue Mountains to save the failing oxen and give birth on the other side to a new baby?

Where is the woman who could labor sixteen hours a day and then upbraid herself in her detailed and intelligent journal: "My mind is so cumbered with a deluge of little corroding cares that all I can think about is 'What shall we eat and what shall we drink and wherewithal shall we be clothed!' My leanness! Oh, my leanness!"

Where is the woman who could mend a roof in a high wind, find substitutes for Thanksgiving mincemeat, make a suit of deer hide with clumsy needles, bear a baby every other year, and still find the interest and the energy to read philosophy, press plants, collect stones, stuff animals, learn an Indian language, write interesting discursive letters, keep a detailed diary? What accounts for the differences in feminine conduct between yesterday and today? Is it simply that pioneer life offered a chance for women to exhibit their fundamental qualities? Was it that, faced with absolute and imminent necessities which there was no way to dodge, dissemble, or escape, a woman grew to her full stature and thus became a heroine for posterity, though in her own eyes her conduct might appear so commonplace as to be unworthy of comment?

In the front of an old book about pioneers there is a crude drawing of a woman in a sunbonnet standing on the top of a mountain. Behind her and ahead are the plodding oxen drawing the prairie schooners. Says the caption: "Woman, yes, woman, has come over the top of the world."

It is interesting to speculate what the effect would have been on the women marching westward into the unknown America of the forties, the fifties, and the sixties had there been photographers, gossip columnists, and staff members of women's magazines to observe them at given points along the route: at Independence, Missouri, for instance, where they began the journey toward the limitless horizon; on the other side of the Platte, where many a new widow would have turned back had there been anyone to accompany her; or finally on the crest of the Continental Divide with the fabled hardships supposedly now behind them.

When woman set out on her great adventure, there were no paid observers to cheapen her glory by making her self-conscious in the moment of her greatness. When she came to the crest of the last mountain she simply walked on down the sunset side of its slope and took up her life and its new problems in the unknown valley below.

Perhaps, symbolically, the real test of women's inherent qualities has come in the valley on the other side of the mountains she crossed during the last century. Life in this valley has become, in certain ways, too easy to challenge her. The modern woman has been accused of surfeiting herself on the sweets of liberty until she has no taste for the simple bread-and-butter fare of hard work and equal responsibility. The pioneer woman won her fight for freedom and equality by enduring with men the same deprivations and hardships. Her sacrifice and her trial became her opportunity for advancement. This was the mountain she crossed. All the privileges that women accept as their rights today were won for them by the Narcissa Whitmans, the Mary Walkers, Abigail Duniways, and Bethenia Owenses of the world. These women all fought to grow to their full powers against heavy odds: hard, inescapable, physical work, and frequently chronic disease.

The first women west paid a price to get to the farthest shoreline of this country and to dominate the wilderness after they got there. The price they paid was high. The pioneer woman's experience is often made to appear glamorous by those who know the least about it. The facts are that Mary Walker lost her mind, and Narcissa Whitman was miserably unhappy, maladjusted to her life of constant sacrifice. Mrs. Eells was always "ailing," Eliza Spalding forever "poorly." For one Samantha Trout, facing it all with bovine equanimity, there were a dozen briefly articulate America Rollins Butlers, confiding to a diary their frantic need of human companionship. Yet, taken as a type, the pioneer woman did what she did without fanfare or self-pity. She commands our most sincere respect for her fortitude and gallantry. But a great part of this fortitude and gallantry grew out of the collective experience in which she was sharing. She was sustained and strengthened by the very fact that she was a pioneer, that she was playing a significant part in a major American experience — the conquering of the last frontier.

We tend to look back enviously on pioneer days because we see in historical retrospect how full of meaning was the life then lived. These people were making a wild land habitable, pushing back inch by inch the wilderness, with their wagon roads, schoolhouses, and churches. They were helping to expand the world. They were moving constantly toward a fuller and easier life. They were making their own future.

What operated among the best of the pioneers was true democracy, with men and women sharing life equally. This period was of short duration in the history of America. For even before World War II — which brought the fact glaringly into the open — men and women had long since ceased to share life equally. They were, indeed, moving farther and farther apart with every passing year. Each, in the main, was doing his job separated from the other — the man outside the home entirely, the woman in it entirely. They had no common meeting-ground — not even in their children, which were the sole concern of the woman. World War II brought new developments to that economic and psychological unit the American home. These changes were disturbing ones to conservative people

[191]

worried about the preservation of familiar ways of life. Women began going out of the home into the world in ever increasing numbers. And when they faced the difficulties of the double demands of home-maker and job-holder, the intelligent ones began to cry out for a modern reorganization of an essentially outmoded institution. They began to ask where were the crèches, the kindergartens, the factory nurseries that women working in industry in a time of crisis could expect, for instance, in a country like Russia.

America, under the stress of war, urged women to enter factories and lend a hand in vital production. Women, on the whole, responded with an alacrity that showed as much as any single thing their wish to escape from the isolated monotony of housework. To be sure, they knew they would work just as hard in a factory as they had at home, but they would get a definite wage for their labor, and they would not be cut off from their fellows. Not to be "cut off" — that was perhaps the most important point. For the first time married women in large numbers were forced to think, on their own, about wages, hours, unions, working conditions — all the problems of the modern industrial world, which up to then they had known only indirectly and hazily through their men. At the same time a certain percentage of men who took over, from necessity, some household tasks of their absent wives got a glimpse into the inner workings of this alien sphere.

When women fresh from years of housework got a first-hand view of industry's efficiency and standardization, they could not but realize that the central unit of national life — the American home — was still geared to an old way of life, to a past tempo. How stupid, for instance, for twenty tired women to go home from their jobs to struggle with twenty separate meals instead of turning for food to a community kitchen! How inconsistent the demand made by a country for more women in factories and offices when no attempt was made on a large scale to solve the problem of what to do with the children of these women!

OVER THE TOP OF THE WORLD

Long ago Abigail Scott Duniway made a wise and cynical remark about women in the Pacific Northwest. She said that more of them would have a chance to lead lives of general service and fulfill their inner drives because they had inexpensive Chinese servants who were willing — happy, even — to do housework. This condition was unfortunately of brief duration. The expulsion of the Chinese from the West coast is an old and familiar story. Mrs. Duniway's remark is only included here because it makes a point. She was in a position to make her remark, to write her book, and to deliver her speeches as she traveled the length and breadth of the country because she had freed herself of domestic drudgery by a long hard climb. She could afford, on her own, to pay for domestic help.

Domestic help is the old solution to the problem of women's dissatisfaction. It is not the new solution. The reason for the alleged discontent, laziness, parasitism, and neuroticism of the American woman-in-the-home is that — unlike the pioneer woman — she feels that the way she lives her life is no longer necessary, therefore no longer meaningful. In spite of all the highly lauded modern gadgets (which only a small percentage of American homes actually have) the American woman is still living in the nineteenth century. And subconsciously she knows it.

The characteristic quality of the pioneer was his willingness to leave the known and go out bravely toward the unknown. The idea of change held no terrors for him. Profound changes are now taking place in our way of life. These changes are overdue if we are to continue as a pioneering people. If we are truly to demonstrate democracy, men and women will have to do it together. A "return to the home" is not necessarily the inevitable answer. Perhaps we must re-examine the home before we take refuge in a slogan that can have, in fact, an ominously fascist ring. Back to the home! cried Germany and Japan. Your womb must be your life, woman, if we are to conquer the world! The pioneer women who conquered their world by the living force of "feminine" ideas disprove the argument that

[193]

physical violence and the flesh-and-blood sacrifice are the only way to demonstrate the truth of a given point of view.

Answers to problems as great as the relationship between men and women and their joint endeavors to establish a truly democratic way of life are not easily come by, nor easily followed when found. Life is not a riddle to be solved in abstract terms, but an experience known only in the day-by-day living of it. This much is certain: Women must now, as Abigail Duniway reminded them, pay to the future the debt they owe the past. They must join together to make possible the next step in their emergence as whole creatures. They must put their mind to the solving of the release of woman's energies from a stale round of nineteenth-century chores so that she may function more intelligently as a wife and mother, or as a worker in the world if that is her choice. There should be, as a matter of fact, no need for any choice. There should no longer be the necessity of having one experience only at the expense of another.

Mary Walker, alone in a primitive environment, had to accept her household drudgery and fit in her mental activities as best she could around this drudgery. This was so inescapably true that she never questioned it. The twentieth-century Mary Walker knows, however, that society could organize the home very differently if it wished to; could take a lesson from industry in large-scale handling of the ever recurrent, boring, mind-dulling round of solitary household tasks which accounts in large measure for the American woman's addiction to the dope of radio's soap operas.

It is up to woman to take hold of her own problem and solve it. No one is going to do it for her.

There is more to women's contemporary problem than this, however. Freedom of action in the democratic sense carries responsibility. American women, who won their freedom so short a time before the great universal light of freedom seemed about to flicker and go out over the surface of the earth, must work continually to keep that light alive. If women are to act as free agents in a chaotic and changing world, they must set about fulfilling their grave responsibility to all life with the quiet dignity of a major imperative. Only thus can they attain to the stature of those pioneer females who faced the great task of their generation with a simple courage which makes us look back upon them as heroines.

READING LIST

(This list is not a full bibliography. It is intended for those who may wish to read further in some of the material included in this volume.)

ANTHONY, SUSAN B.: *History of Women Suffrage, 1876–1885*. Fowler & Wills, New York, 1881.

BAGLEY, CLARENCE: *Early Catholic Missions in Old Oregon*. Lowman & Hanford Company, Seattle, 1932.

BAILEY, ROBERT G.: *River of No Return*. Bailey-Blake Printing Co., Lewiston, Idaho, 1935.

BALLOU, ROBERT: *Early Klickitat Valley Days*. Goldendale Sentinel, Goldendale, Washington, 1938.

BELSHAW, MARIA PARSONS: "Diary of a Bride Written on the Trail in 1853." *Oregon Historical Society Quarterly*, Vol. XXXIII.

BINNS, ARCHIE: *The Land Is Bright* (novel). Charles Scribner's Sons, New York, 1939.

BOWDEN, ANGIE BURT: *Early Schools of Washington Territory*. Lowman & Hanford, Seattle, 1935.

DEFENBACH, BYRON: *Red Heroines of the Northwest*. The Caxton Printers, Caldwell, Idaho, 1929.

DONALDSON, THOMAS C.: *Idaho of Yesterday*. The Caxton Printers, Caldwell, Idaho, 1941.

DOUTHIT, MARY OSBORN: *A Souvenir of Western Women*. Portland, Oregon, 1905.

DRURY, CLIFFORD MERRILL: *Henry Harmon Spalding*. The Caxton Printers, Caldwell, Idaho, 1936.

——: *Marcus Whitman, M.D., Pioneer and Martyr*. The Caxton Printers, Caldwell, Idaho, 1937.

——: *Elkanah and Mary Walker, Pioneers among the Spokanes*. The Caxton Printers, Caldwell, Idaho, 1940.

DUNIWAY, ABIGAIL SCOTT: *Path Breaking, an Autobiographical History of the Equal Suffrage Movement in Pacific Coast States*. James, Kerns & Abbott Co., Portland, Oregon, 1914.

Dye, Eva Emery: *The Conquest, the True Story of Lewis & Clark* (fictionized history). A. C. McClurg & Co., Chicago, 1902.

——: *McLoughlin and Old Oregon.* A. C. McClurg & Co., Chicago, 1913.

——: *The Soul of America.* The Press of the Pioneers, New York, 1934.

——: "Woman's Part in the Drama of the Northwest." *Oregon Pioneer Assn. Transactions,* Vol. II, page 36, 22nd Annual Reunion, 1894.

Earle, Alice M.: *Colonial Dames and Goodwives.* The Macmillan Co., New York, 1924.

Emmons, Della Gould: *Sacajawea of the Shoshones.* Binfords & Mort, Portland, Oregon, 1943.

Engle, Flora A. P.: "The Story of the Mercer Expedition." *Washington Historical Quarterly,* Vol. VI, No. 4 (October 1915).

Fuller, George W.: *A History of the Pacific Northwest.* Alfred A. Knopf, New York, 1938.

Gay, Theressa: *Life and Letters of Mrs. Jason Lee of the Oregon Mission.* Binfords & Mort, Portland, Oregon, 1936.

Gedney, Elizabeth: "Cross Section of Life at Fourth Plain." *Oregon Historical Quarterly,* Vol. XLIII.

Geer, Mrs. Elizabeth Dixon Smith: "Diary Written on the Oregon Trail in 1847." *Transactions of the 35th Annual Reunion of the Oregon Pioneer Association,* Portland, June 19, 1907.

Geer, T. T.: *Fifty Years in Oregon.* The Neale Publishing Company, New York, 1912.

Hebard, Grace Raymond: *Sacajawea.* The Arthur H. Clark Co., Glendale, California, 1933.

Idaho Lore. Federal Writers Project, The Caxton Printers, Caldwell, Idaho, 1939.

In Harvest Fields by Sunset Shores, the Work of the Sisters of Notre Dame on the Pacific Coast, by a member of the Congregation. Gilmartin, San Francisco, 1926.

JUDSON, PHOEBE GOODELL: *A Pioneer's Search for an Ideal Home* (1853). Bellingham, Washington, 1925.

JONES, NARD: *Scarlet Petticoat* (novel). Dodd, Mead & Company, New York, 1941.

KELLY, FANNY: *Narrative of My Captivity among the Sioux Indians.* Philadelphia, 1872.

LEIGHTON, CAROLINE: *Life at Puget Sound. 1865–1881.* Lee and Shepard, Boston; Charles T. Dillingham, New York; 1884.

Notice sur la territoire et sur la mission de l'Oregon suivie du quelques lettres des Sœurs de Notre Dame. Brussels, Belgium, 1847.

OWENS-ADAIR, DR. BETHENIA: *Some of Her Life Experiences.* Mann & Beach, Portland, Oregon, 1906.

PADEN, IRENE D.: *Wake of the Prairie Schooner.* The Macmillan Co., New York, 1943.

PORTER, KENNETH W.: "Jane Barnes, First White Woman in Oregon." *Oregon Historical Quarterly,* Vol. XXXI, No. 2, p. 125 (June 1930).

PURCELL, POLLY JANE: *Autobiography and Reminiscences.* Freewater, Oregon, 1922.

REID, AGNES JUST: *Letters of Long Ago.* The Caxton Printers, Caldwell, Idaho, 1936.

STOLL, WILLIAM T.: *Silver Strike, the True Story of Silver Mining in the Cœur d'Alenes.* Little, Brown & Company, Boston, 1932.

THWAITES, REUBEN GOLD, ed.: *Early Western Travels, 1748–1846: A Series of Annotated Reprints of Some of the Best and Rarest Contemporary Volumes of Travel . . . during the Period of Early American Settlement.* The A. H. Clark Co., Cleveland, 1904–7.

——: *Original Journals of the Lewis and Clark Expedition,* Dodd, Mead & Co., New York, 1904.

Told by the Pioneers; Reminiscences of Pioneer Life in Washington. 3 vols. W.P.A. Sponsored Federal Project, 1936–8.

VICTOR, FRANCES FULLER: *The New Penelope and Other Stories and Poems.* A. L. Bancroft & Co., San Francisco, 1877.

——: *The River of the West. Life and Adventures in the Rocky*

Mountains and Oregon. R. W. Bliss & Co., Hartford; R. J. Trumbull & Co., San Francisco; 1870.

WARREN, ELIZA SPALDING: *Memoirs of the West.* Portland, Oregon, 1916.

WATTS, ROBERTA FRYE: *Four Wagons West.* Binfords & Mort, Portland, Oregon, 1931.

WHITMAN, NARCISSA: "Diary." *Oregon Historical Quarterly,* June, September, and December 1936, and *Transactions of the Oregon Pioneer Association,* 1891.